Solving the Assessment Puzzle Piece by Piece

Revised Edition

Carolyn Coil
Dodie Merritt

Pieces of Learning

Cover by John Steele
1112 N Carbon St, STE A
Marion IL 62959

www.piecesoflearning.com

CLC0470
ISBN 978-1-934358-87-0

2018 Printing—Now with ESSA

Table of Contents

Acknowledgements

With appreciation for all of my DeKalb County, Georgia, graduate students -

For those who encouraged me to learn about assessment and teach the course *Educational Assessment and Measurement*

For those who learned about rubrics and checklists, developed them and applied what they learned in their classrooms. You are my "living laboratory!"

– Carolyn Coil

In appreciation and in recognition of -

My colleagues in the Genoa-Kingston School district, Genoa, IL, who made developing effective rubrics authentic and fun

Jim Curry's English teacher who coined the term "NSH" or "Not So Hot"

Family and friends for their understanding, love, and support always!

– Dodie Merritt

Chapter 1
Introduction

What Does It All Mean and Why Do We Do It Anyway?

Ms. Weeks was drowning in a sea of papers to grade. She knew her students would demand to know their grades immediately, but she felt overwhelmed. Not only did she have to grade the papers, she also had to enter the numbers in her school's computerized grading program. "We live and die by numbers and points and scores and data," she thought. "How much does this show us what kids actually learn?"

The school principal, Mr. Vasquez, was worried about test scores. The standardized test the district had been using for several years had just been re-normed, and the superintendent didn't want to see test scores drop. His school was successfully using many types of alternative assessments, but he didn't know how student progress might be reflected in the re-normed test. He did know that his school and all others in the district would be evaluated based on test scores. "Test scores are everything in this district," he told his teachers.

How, why, and what we assess are some of the most pressing issues, questions, and concerns in education today. Indeed, if assessment is the tail and curriculum the dog, we certainly often have a case of the tail wagging the dog! Many educators are deeply concerned about this issue yet feel lost or confused in the competing requirements, needs, and demands they hear from students, parents, administrators, state and federal government, and the public at large.

This book is written for teachers, administrators, and other practitioners who are not assessment experts but who need to know and understand the basics of assessment and what is being required of them. In this book, we take a broad look at assessment and what it means for today's educators. All facets of assessment, from assessment terminology to standardized tests, from portfolios to report cards, from rubrics to standards and benchmarks are considered. We hope it will clarify assessment issues for you and will make them easier to deal with and understand.

As a result of reading this book, you will:

- Comprehend basic assessment terminology and uses for assessments
- Understand the advantages and disadvantages of standardized tests and alternative assessment measures
- Understand ways data can drive instruction
- Know the purposes and functions of standards and benchmarks
- Know how to use pre-assessment, formative assessment and summative assessment
- Know how to write rubrics and other forms of alternative assessments
- Understand the purpose, effects, and impact of federal mandates concerning assessment
- See numerous samples of rubrics written by classroom teachers
- Find a variety of ways to report student progress

On the next page you will see the *Bottle of Water* activity. I have used this activity in many of my assessment workshops in order to introduce four basic terms that are used over and over again (often interchangeably though they shouldn't be) when we discuss educational assessment issues. These are:

- Assess
- Measure
- Test
- Evaluate

This activity purposely does not directly relate to education and, in fact, is particularly helpful for that very reason. Sometimes when we step back from our area of concentration and expertise and see issues in a broader perspective, it helps us put them into focus more easily. That is what this activity is intended to achieve. You may do the activity by yourself, or you can discuss it in a group setting so that you can brainstorm together and debate different points of view.

Do the activity before looking at subsequent pages for explanations and a discussion of the four terms.

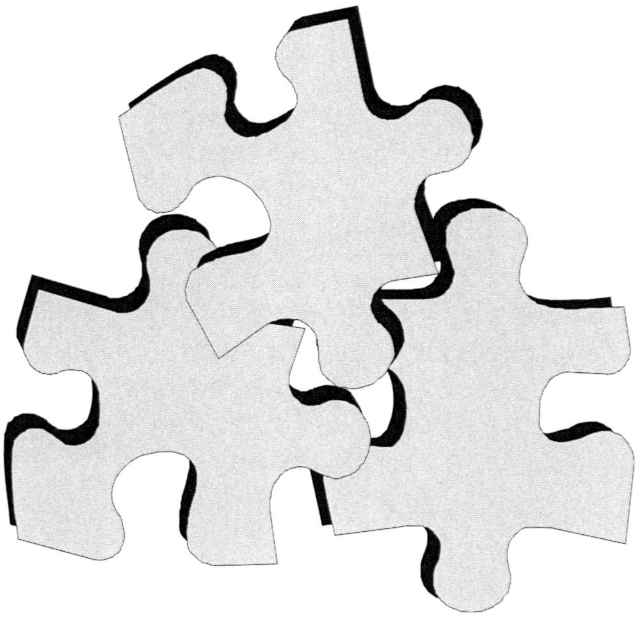

Bottle of Water Activity

A bottle of water can teach us a great deal about assessment and the terminology we use when discussing it. Get a bottle of water and put it in front of you as you do this activity. Consider the bottle of water as you discuss each of the following:

How would you:

1. Assess it?

2. Measure it?

3. Test it?

4. Evaluate it?

What are the differences in these four terms?

In educational assessment, what do you do when you measure something?

How can you assess <u>without</u> measuring?

Reproducible

Thinking About the *Bottle of Water* Activity

Now that you've completed the *Bottle of Water* activity, you might like to read my ideas and the ideas of other teachers as they did this activity.

Assess

> *I would use a variety of techniques to find out about distinct characteristics or properties of the liquid, such as quality, purity, density, clarity, composition. I would observe it using all of my senses. I'd taste it, smell it, stir it, look at it or use it. This would give me the opportunities I need to gather the data necessary to make a conclusion. -- Workshop participant*

Assessment is the broad term that encompasses all the others. Considering assessing a bottle of water, we would need to collect and gather information and data from a wide variety of sources, settings, and circumstances. We might observe and determine what its uses are.

We could design a checklist and look at as many different factors as possible, using the five senses to observe the properties of water and check them off. The checklist might include the following questions:

- Is it a liquid?
- What is its color and clarity?
- Is it hot or cold?
- What does it smell like?
- Is it safe to drink?
- Shall I taste it?
- What does it taste like?

In our process of assessment, we might want to analyze the label as well as specific parts and qualities of the water, then combine and integrate our new findings with previous knowledge about the properties and characteristics of water. Then we would have the information we need to make a knowledgeable assessment.

Assessment can be any method through which one gathers data to find out about something. Assessing something means you may measure it or evaluate it. It means having a broad viewpoint and finding out much more information than test results can give. Assessment means using all the information and data gathered, along with previous knowledge, in order to make a decision about the whole.

Measure

> *I would look at the label to determine how much water is in the bottle, how much it weighs, and the amount of each chemical in the water. Then I would systematically collect, quantify, and make an ordered list of all the properties of the water. —Middle school science teacher*

Measurement nearly always means expressing information in the form of a number or quantity. These, in turn, provide specific data for assessments. Measurement quantifies learning. It is systematic and uses some type of predetermined standard with specific defined criteria.

Measurement includes factors such as a numerical score, quantitative analysis, knowing how many, and perhaps a percentage or percentile ranking. When you measure something, you examine specific parts or qualities and then use a standard for determining some type of numerical value or rank.

When something is measured, it is important that everyone be in agreement regarding what the numbers actually mean. If I told you the score, rank, or rating is 70, this would have no meaning unless I also told you the significance of the number. Is it a percentage? a percentile? a class ranking? a golf score? Numbers in and of themselves have no value and no purpose in measurement. It is only when the standard of measurement is known that numbers become important.

In the *Bottle of Water* activity, we could measure the water in many ways. However, these measurements would tell us little if we didn't know the significance behind the numbers themselves. The same is true of the measurements we use in the classroom.

Test

> *You would most likely test the water in the bottle for specific properties, like its ph content or its chemical make-up. You could also test it to see if it is drinkable or not and whether it has harmful micro-organisms. I would probably put drops of water onto slides and examine them under the microscope.*
>
> *— Teacher, 5th grade*

When I've done this activity with my graduate students or in a workshop, "test" is the word that many participants miss in terms of its real meaning and significance. The most important thing about any test is that it involves taking a sample and assuming it is representative of the whole.

To test the water, we would need to establish the specific purpose for the test. After the purpose was established and the testing procedures set, we would go ahead and conduct the test. We might even do the same test several times in order to make sure our results were accurate. But one thing is certain. We would not pour the entire bottle of water onto the microscope slide in order to conduct the test. We would take several samples, but we wouldn't use the whole thing!

The same is true with medical tests. When someone goes to the doctor or hospital for a blood test, a few drops or perhaps a few vials of blood are taken. It is a given that no one would go for a blood test if they were going to drain all the blood from your body in order to do the test!

When I look at the function of tests in schools, however, I feel this is exactly what is happening. Instead of the test being *one* sample of student work and *one* sample of students' learning of the curriculum, in many schools the test has *become* the entire curriculum! Many teachers are told that if it's not on the test it is not important to teach it. Teaching units and daily lesson plans are written based only on the standards that are tested. Important and enriching classroom activities are being eliminated because they aren't being tested. How did we get to the point in education where we assume the test drives the entire curriculum? This is not what a test is supposed to do!

When I was a classroom teacher, my students would sometimes come to me after a test and complain, "You didn't ask all the stuff I studied!" My response was always, "Did you know the answers to the questions I did ask?" Most of the time my students grudgingly admitted that they did. This was always my cue that my test was fair. I never wanted my test to test *everything they knew.* I did want it to be a fair sampling of what they studied and what they had learned. In my mind, this is the true function of a test, whether it is a teacher-made or a standardized test.

We will examine standardized educational testing more thoroughly in Chapter 4.

Evaluate

> *When evaluating, I would focus on forming a judgment about the bottle of water. In my evaluation I could ask several questions: Was the water the temperature I prefer? Was it drinkable? Was it flavored? Should I try to generalize what I've learned to other bottles of water? These and other similar questions would form the basis for my evaluation. —High school teacher*

To evaluate means to make a value judgment based on a set of specific criteria. Evaluation is often done by integrating new data with what you already know. In our bottle of water example, we might evaluate by making judgments and decisions about the nature of the water based on the knowledge we have gained through our tests, measurements, and other assessments and based on what we know about water from our general knowledge and past experiences.

Many times, worth, value, or quality is determined by comparisons and by the interpretation of results and data. Because of this, we would need to consider all the data in order to make a valid judgment about the water.

Because evaluation is a judgment call, it may be more subjective than the other three terms we have considered. This is particularly true in educational assessment. We are not evaluating an object such as a bottle of water but instead are evaluating human beings.

In an age of intense educational accountability, it is important that we maintain a balance so that we don't go overboard quantifying everything by the numbers and evaluating every form of human behavior and interaction. At the same time, we have to make sure our value judgments are not clouded by bias, personal preference, or undocumented assessments based on good intentions.

Similarities in and uses of the four terms

These four terms — assessment, testing, measuring, and evaluating   overlap. They all depend on each other. It is very difficult to do one without eventually including the others. Testing and measurement are components of assessment. Evaluation is the process of making judgments and decisions using tests, measurements, and other assessments as the basis of one's decision making.

We need to be certain our measurements and subsequent evaluations are understood by all who examine them. Traditionally, when we measure something in educational assessment, we compare a score to a given standard by using a numerical grade that is translated into a letter grade. While these letter grades are nearly universally understood, they are not standardized. One teacher's **A** could be another teacher's **C**.

Many schools now use standards-based report cards. These are designed to show student progress over time on specific grade-level state standards, They are usually developed at the district level and reflect a performance range in mastering the standards from "below level" to "exceeds."

In schools we collect information and measurements in a variety of ways. We use multiple choice tests, teacher-made tests, standardized tests, and essay tests, each with a numerical scoring key. We use checklists, charts, graphs, teacher observations with numerical scales, classwork grades, homework grades, and rubrics with numbers. All of these are necessary and important measurement tools.

As educators, we also assess without measuring. This type of assessment includes teacher observations, interaction with peers, performances, and portfolios. We also use student products, question and answer sessions, data without numbers, and co-operative group discussions. We may have students work on problems involving real life situations and observe their ability to apply knowledge across the curriculum. With these assessments, we often rely on anecdotal records or verbal descriptions as alternatives to specific numeric measurements.

Not everything that counts can be counted,
and not everything that can be counted counts.
– William Bruce Cameron

Why Assess?

If we assess it, everyone believes it's important!

Tracey, a fifth grade teacher, was feeling particularly discouraged after spending her whole weekend grading papers and creating a unit test to give to her students during the upcoming week. "Why do I bother to assess my students anyway?" she thought. "Isn't it enough just to teach them without having to grade all those papers, give test after test, create rubrics for projects, and then somehow count up all those points at report card time? I'd like to take this grade book and throw it away! Assessment is just a lot of unnecessary paperwork."

10 Basic Purposes of Assessment

1. Selecting, clarifying, and evaluating educational objectives and outcomes

Objectives frequently become much clearer when educators deal with assessment issues. When we use assessment data well, we take a comprehensive look at student outcomes and then match our teaching objectives to the students' needs. We may ask ourselves, "What is really important for students to know and to be able to do? What are the essentials?" Our objectives must also be clearly stated to the students. This is best done before instruction begins. When we look at what we will assess, we know where our focus and emphasis should be.

2. Planning instruction

When used correctly, assessment can be a wonderful instructional tool. It can help us find out what our students already know. We can then use this information and plan instruction based on it. This involves pre-testing, identifying strengths and weaknesses, and knowing when remediation or acceleration is needed and for what they are needed. Using assessment in this way can make our teaching more efficient and effective.

Assessment gives us the information we need to implement ongoing differentiated instruction. It allows us to evaluate student progress and plan instruction accordingly. By assessing our students' readiness levels and learning profiles, we can better plan a wider range of classroom activities and educational experiences to meet all of their needs.

3. Evaluating student work

One of the most obvious purposes of assessment is that it gives us a way to evaluate students and make judgments about their work on a regular basis. Teachers struggle to find ways to do this fairly and accurately. Establishing specific standards-based criteria for evaluation is a critical first step. From this criteria we can determine more concrete assessment tools such as points, scores, percentages, or letter grades. Student work, especially projects and performances, may also be evaluated using rubrics, checklists, observation logs, etc.

4. Reporting and comparing student progress

Parents want to know how well their child is doing. Most are interested in knowing their child's position relative to state educational standards. They may also want to know how their child compares to others in the school, district, state, or nation. School boards, administrators, and the media often want to use student assessment to compare student progress between one year and another or between one school and another. Therefore, it is important that we find ways to inform students, their parents, and others about student progress.

For individual students, the most efficient way to communicate this information is through grades on a progress report or report card. Report card grades, however, are more than just interesting information! They determine grade point averages and class rankings that are unbelievably significant to many students and their parents. Even with standards-based report cards, we need to remember that grades are just one indicator of student progress.

For a more generalized look at student progress, we use various types of standardized test scores. They provide views of students' positions as they relate to state and national educational standards. From these scores, comparisons can be made from year to year, from student to student, or from school to school.

Other assessment methods may provide different perspectives about student progress. Student-led conferences, parent-teacher conferences, portfolios of student work that demonstrate progress over time, weekly or monthly progress reports, videos of student performances, student journals, and learning logs are examples. Assessing students in all of these ways can help us ascertain a student's standing and lead us to the next step by showing what that student can do to improve or to maintain progress.

5. Counseling

Students constantly need guidance in the academic realm as well as in their personal growth and affective skills. Some have severe social or emotional problems while others may struggle academically. Assessment instruments give us a way to identify which students are contending with emotional or psychological problems and can help us determine how to best help these students. Psychological tests, vocational preference tests, checklists assessing strengths and weaknesses, and student questionnaires are some of the instruments we can use to help us deal with these problems and counsel students effectively.

Student self-assessment is an excellent counseling tool. It helps students assess their own strengths and weaknesses in the context of academics, career planning, and personal growth. Students who are aware of their own strengths and weaknesses learn to make adjustments and choices that are beneficial for their development throughout their lives.

6. Motivating and encouraging students

Assessments provide motivation and encouragement for many students. Procrastinators need due dates and an assurance their work will be examined and assessed by the teacher. If work was never assessed, and everyone was guaranteed to receive the same grade no matter what work they had done, many students would stop working as hard as they do, and some would stop working altogether!

Without some type of assessment, most students would think, "Why bother?" Others would become very resentful because they were working so much harder than others yet did not get any particular credit or recognition for doing so. The Communist economic system collapsed for similar reasons. Perhaps it is human nature to be motivated by getting rewards for hard work. Assessment serves this purpose for many students.

Assessment also serves as a motivator when students can see their progress and accomplishments. For a student who is discouraged and feels unmotivated, looking at past performance and seeing how much improvement has been made can be a great encourager. Assessment makes this progress more readily observable, quantifiable, and obvious.

Finally, assessment helps us predict future performance. Students are often motivated by goals for the future, and various types of assessments help point the way to future possibilities. This can be a tremendous inspiration to some students.

7. Giving special recognition to students

Assessments give us data to use when choosing students to recognize for outstanding accomplishments. Selecting students for special honors such as membership in Beta Club or the National Honor Society includes assessing them in a number of different ways based on established criteria. This assures that the selection process is fair and unbiased.

Special recognition is often given to students for outstanding products or performances. Science fair winners, first chair in band, and first place in a writing contest are all chosen through various types of project or performance assessments. Gathering assessment data helps us be fair evaluators so that appropriate recognition can be given.

8. Selecting students for special programs or instruction

In general, the criteria for entry into special programs are set by district, state, or federal regulations. The data from various assessment instruments helps us see which students meet the criteria so they can be placed in appropriate learning environments. Identification procedures for gifted or special education students generally require that students be assessed in specific ways. This is significant because accurately assessing and selecting students for special programs allows them to interact with others that are functioning on the same ability level as well as receive targeted and appropriate instruction.

9. Evaluating program effectiveness

Assessment can be used to improve a program or to judge its worth and effectiveness. It is a good way to make sure a program is meeting student needs and its stated goals and objectives. Assessments often give validity to programs by documenting innovative teaching strategies and techniques, student growth, parental involvement, changes in student attitudes, etc.

Peer review is sometimes a feature of this type of evaluation. Programs are evaluated by teachers from another district in the same state. Teachers are evaluated by their peers based on standards developed by teachers and the school district. When done well, this type of review and evaluation helps us make positive changes and encourages us to keep doing the things that are working well.

10. Holding schools accountable

"How good a job are you doing?" is the central question of accountability, but this is often fraught with questions and misunderstandings. Accountability includes standards, standardized test scores, performance indicators such as dropout rates, school attendance, and rewards and sanctions. Test scores, student outcomes, and the other factors mentioned above are valuable information but are not automatic verdicts of good or poor teaching. Should teachers be held accountable for their students' performance or only for providing good teaching?

President Obama signed the Every Student Succeeds Act (ESSA) into law on December 10, 2015. It replaced No Child Left Behind (NCLB) whose prescriptive accountability requirements had become increasingly unworkable for schools and educators. ESSA gives more decision-making power back to the states, with accountability being state-driven and based on multiple measures. The ESSA maintains the federal mandate on public school districts to give standardized tests to students in the third through eighth grades and once in high school for accountability purposes. However, it leaves it up to the states to decide how to deal with the lowest-performing schools.

Under ESSA, schools are still accountable for student performance, but states can determine the nuances of how that will take place. School districts must ensure that at least 95 percent of students participate, and disaggregate data based on students' race, income, and disability status. For accountability purposes, they can use other factors in addition to testing to assess student performance, and the details of how the testing happens and how the scores are interpreted are up to states.

The current accountability movement sometimes limits teachers' control over curriculum and instruction and at times seems distrustful of teachers' professional ability to assess student performance and growth. However, using assessment data to hold schools accountable can serve many positive purposes. It can help teachers target skills and outcomes. It gives us specific standards and benchmarks to work toward. In any case, assessment data should not be used to punish teachers, administrators, or schools who are working as hard as they can, sometimes under extremely difficult circumstances.

Why Assess?
Teacher Reflection Page

1. Review the 10 purposes for assessment listed and discussed in this chapter. In the space below, write the three most significant for you and a sentence or two explaining why these three are particularly important. If possible, discuss your top three with a colleague.

   1. ______________________________

      ____

      ____

   2. ______________________________

      ____

      ____

   3. ______________________________

      ____

      ____

2. What other purposes do you see for assessment?

3. Tracey, the teacher quoted at the beginning of this section, says: *"Assessment is just a lot of unnecessary paperwork."* Do you agree or disagree? Why or why not?

Chapter 2
Assessment Terminology

50 Terms to Understand So You Can Talk Like an Assessment Expert

This chapter establishes a common language for this book and should be useful in any discussions you have about assessment. Its purpose is to acquaint those of you who are not familiar with assessment terminology with the words used both by experts in the field as well as by those who think they understand educational assessment but often do not. Terms mean different things to different people. Misunderstandings caused by misinterpreting the meanings of specific terms may result in confusion and conflict. Uses of assessment data for purposes for which it was not intended become clear when you understand the terminology. The definitions have been written in an understandable, user-friendly fashion with a minimum of jargon. Make sure you fully comprehend each of these terms. This will be a great advantage to you in any discussion you have about educational assessment, measurement, or testing.

1. **accountability** - Responsibility for student learning based on agreed-upon criteria such as rubrics or test scores. It includes being responsible for and being able to document results. In most systems of educational accountability, teachers are responsible for what they teach and what the child learns. When curriculum is diverse and flexible and involves higher-level thinking skills, it is more difficult to measure accountability via standardized testing.

2. **achievement test** - A type of test that measures what has been taught and learned and the extent to which an individual has achieved or mastered a set of defined objectives or learning outcomes, usually acquired as the result of instruction or schooling. This test should be administered after the program, unit of work, or experience has been completed. Often it is a written standardized test that measures the information, knowledge, or skills acquired in certain subject areas and is used to judge specific academic abilities. These tests are more valid and reliable when the test objectives are aligned with what has actually been taught. When this type of test is based on grade level work, it may not show the actual achievement of gifted and high-ability students because these students often hit the test ceiling, and there is no way to measure the height of their achievement. Examples: Iowa Test of Basic Skills, California Achievement Test, many state-developed standardized tests given at various grade levels.

3. Adequate Yearly Progress (AYP) - This was the federal measurement of student progress under No Child Left Behind. The Every Student Succeeds Act (ESSA) repealed this measurement and replaced it with the requirement that all states develop their own accountability systems and come up with a plan to identify and support the lowest performing 5% of schools.

4. **aptitude** - A combination of natural and acquired talents, interests, and/or abilities that a student may innately possess or that he/she may have learned. These usually indicate ability to learn more and develop proficiency in a given area, subject, or skill.

5. **aptitude test** - A test that measures a person's abilities in something he has not been taught. It generally measures or predicts what a student will be able to do in the future and the likely effects of future learning experiences. Thus, it may predict future behavior, achievements, or performance by measuring general abilities, knowledge, and problem solving skills. These tests are often used to measure general intelligence or mental ability and to predict the likelihood of an individual's benefiting from a certain type of educational or training program. Examples include IQ tests that predict how well a student will do in school and SAT's, ACT's, and GRE's that predict success in college or graduate school.

6. **assessment** - A broad, general term used to describe any systematic approach or plan for gathering, using, synthesizing, and evaluating data to find out more about a student; to establish effectiveness of curriculum, instruction, and program; to determine strengths and weaknesses; to appraise ability and performance; and/or to see what has been learned.

7. **average** - Mathematically, the sum of a group of numbers divided by the amount of numbers. This term is also used to describe the center, the normal, or the general level of knowledge which is minimally acceptable. On report cards, a grade of 'C' usually indicates average. In schools, the desire is often expressed to be above average.

8. **battery** - A set of tests that were normed or standardized on the same group of students so that the results of each test can be compared to one another. Often these tests measure similar kinds of abilities and skills. Also used to indicate any series of tests given together; each test in the series gives different types of information.

9. **benchmarks** - A progression showing the steps, guideposts, or reasonable expectations indicating what students are capable of learning and what they should know and be able to do at different ages and grade levels in regard to standards. They often provide the framework for teaching and assessing key concepts and skills, because they are usually more specific and concrete than standards.

10. **bias** - A leaning or inclination giving an unfair advantage or disadvantage. An undesirable characteristic of tests in which factors unrelated to the test influence the scores. Therefore, the content of test items discriminates in favor of or against certain students or groups of students because of their experiences, race, gender, cultural exposure, economic status, etc. An error in content, administration, and/or interpretation built into the system that contributes to a statistical difference between groups or types of people.

11. **ceiling** - The upper limit that can be measured by a given test or assessment. Individuals are said to have reached this point when their abilities exceed the highest performance level at which the test can make reliable discriminations. Test ceilings create problems in measuring the progress of gifted/high achieving students who may hit the ceiling before beginning a unit of study or a school year.

12. **consistency** - Doing the same thing every time. Accuracy and predictability in measurement over a period of time with different students and different scorers in different environments.

13. **content validity** - Describes the degree to which a given test measures what it says it is measuring.

14. **correlation** - A relationship, correspondence, or connection between any two things. This is not a cause and effect relationship; two items may be strongly correlated without one causing the other.

15. **criterion-referenced assessment** - An assessment that measures progress toward mastery of a given set of objectives, outcomes, or skills. This measurement does not compare one person's score to the scores of the rest of the group. Instead, it is an objective measure of mastery tied to specific skills and objectives that are measured based on predetermined standards or criteria. Each individual is judged on how well he achieves the criteria, with an emphasis on performance relative to an absolute standard.

16. **deviation** - The extent to which a score differs from a certain reference point, usually the norm, midpoint, or average.

17. **diagnostic test** - Test that assesses specific skills to determine specific individual strengths and weaknesses, usually in reading and/or math. This type of test should be used by teachers to guide them in planning instruction based on student needs. Such tests should be tied to curriculum and content objectives.

18. **evaluation** - Process of gathering and using qualitative and quantitative data to make a judgment of value, worth, merit, or effectiveness. This can be for an individual student, group, class, grade level, department, school, school district, or program.

19. **formative assessment** - Information and data gathered is used to improve, modify, or revise a program, curriculum, or unit of instruction. This type of assessment is helpful because it provides ongoing feedback to students and can clarify misconceptions during the learning process.

20. **grade equivalent** - Theoretically, an average score at a given grade level. This score relates a student's raw score to the average scores obtained by norming groups at different grade levels. This score is often greatly distorted because there are so many variations in what is actually taught at each grade level.

21. **high-stakes test** - A test whose results will have a significant impact on the life of the student, teacher, administration, and/or school. Often the scores determine eligibility for programs, school admission, school rankings, etc. Examples include graduation tests, the SAT and ACT tests, end of grade tests, and statewide standardized tests that determine whether a school has met AYP.

22. **intelligence quotient (IQ)** - A number that indicates the ratio of one's mental age to his/her chronological age. The average IQ is thought to be 100. An IQ score is no longer thought to be the sole measure of intelligence, nor is it always a fixed number throughout a person's life. IQ scores can change over time due to a person's ability to learn from experience, to respond quickly in new situations, and to use reasoning and logic to solve problems.

23. **Likert scale** - A numeric rating scale of attitudes or values indicating most to least, strongly agree to strongly disagree, etc. The respondent uses this scale to indicate attitudes about people, places, ideas, concepts, activities, or objects. It is useful in putting a numeric measurement onto qualitative ideas and other things that are hard to measure objectively.

24. **mastery test** - A criterion-referenced test that shows the extent to which a student has mastered a given set of objectives or skills. This assessment gives the teacher information about what the student already knows, what he has learned in a given amount of time, and what he still needs to know.

25. **measurement** - The process of gathering data and quantifying something according to a numerical scale or standard and assigning numbers to processes, events, and objects.

26. **mean** - The average of a set of scores or numbers; the sum divided by the number of scores. Extremes in scores skew the mean. For instance, giving a student a zero has a major effect on his average.

27. **median** - The middle number; the point where there are one-half above and one-half below thus dividing the group into two equal parts; the 50th percentile.

28. **mental age** - The age for which a given score on an intelligence test is considered average or normal.

29. **norm-referenced test** - Includes both standardized and specially constructed intelligence and achievement tests that compare students to one another. Performance of others is the standard by which the student is measured. Scores are put in rank order and are used to measure one person's results as compared to another's. Students who compete with one another for selection when there are a limited number of places may compete via norm-referenced tests.

30. **norms** - Statistics developed by test makers to represent specific populations and how the average person in that population would do on a specific test. Norms may include grade, age, percentile, or standard score and provide a basis for comparison.

31. **objectivity** - Consistency in scoring no matter who the scorer is. As such, it precludes differences of opinion among scorers as to whether responses are to be scored right or wrong. This is much easier to accomplish with a test that has a given correct answer for each item.

32. **percentage** - The number of points or a given part out of 100. The score on many classroom tests as well as report card grades are based on the percentage a student has correct.

33. **percentile** - One of the points on a 99 point scale. Each point reflects the distribution of ranked scores and shows a person's relative standing within a particular group. Your position on the percentile scale shows the percentage of those above and those below you. The percentiles of any given group will therefore show half above the 50th percentile and half below the 50th percentile. Though many people get the terms confused, *percentile* is not the same as a *percentage*. For example, a student could score 95% on a test and be in any percentile depending on the scores of the others in the group.

34. **performance assessment** - Any systematic, evaluative appraisal of a student's ability to perform tasks or do something. Examples include demonstrations, dance recitals, oral reports, cheerleader tryouts, and work samples.

35. **portfolio assessment** - A collection and evaluation of student products and performances selected for inclusion based on agreed-upon criteria. Portfolios generally illustrate a range of abilities and special talents showing growth, self-reflection, and achievement. They may be composed of the student's best work or work that shows improvement over time.

36. progress monitoring - Emphasized in the Response to Intervention (RTI) approach, progress monitoring is a research-based practice used to assess students' academic and behavioral performance and to evaluate the effectiveness of instruction and interventions. Progress monitoring can be completed with individual students, groups of students, or an entire class. To implement progress monitoring, the student's current levels of performance are determined and goals are identified for learning that will take place over time. Student progress is measured on a regular basis, and teaching is adjusted as needed.

37. **quartile** - The division of achievement distribution into four equal parts. The quartile scale is 0-25, 26-50, 51-75 and 76-100. The number of persons per quartile is the same.

38. **range** - The difference between the highest score and the lowest score plus 1.

39. **reliability** - The extent to which scores, tests, programs, or assessments are accurate, dependable, stable, consistent, and free from error over a period of time. This includes the way they are administered, implemented, and scored.

40. **rubric** - A teacher-constructed list of characteristics used as criteria for ranking the quality of students' work along with some type of guide for scoring or grading. Usually this guide describes the criteria along with a numerical range or scale to indicate the degree of quality or mastery shown by the work. There are many different types of rubrics all of which are useful for project or performance assessment.

41. **standard deviation** - A statistical measure of the dispersion in a set of scores, beginning with the mean or average. Usually the standard deviation is a 15 point range. It is used to indicate what percent of scores are higher and lower than the mean.

42. **standardized test** - A systematic sample of student performance obtained under prescribed conditions such as time allotted, verbal instructions required, etc. Such tests are usually developed for state or national use and are norm-referenced in order to provide accurate and meaningful information regarding a student's level of performance relative to others at the same age or grade level. Many of these tests are high-stakes tests, and their scores may be the sole criterion upon which students, teachers, or administrators are judged. Because of this, such tests often take on great importance resulting in curriculum and instruction being aligned to test items and objectives.

43. **standards** - Agreed-upon values used to measure levels of attainment that students should work toward in content, process, performance, or lifelong learning. Specific indicators of what students should know and be able to do as a result of their education.

44. standards-based report card - A standards-based report card lists the most important skills and knowledge students should learn in each subject at a particular grade level relative to the standards. Instead of letter grades, the marks show the progress each student has made toward mastering each standard. Usually there are three or four levels (such as advanced, proficient, basic, and below basic) on the report card.

45. **stanine** - A type of standardized score based on a scale of nine equal units that range from a high of 9 to a low of 1. In general, stanines 1-3 are considered below average, 4-6 are average, and 7-9 above average.

46. student-led conferences - In a student-led conference, the responsibility rests with the student. The teacher facilitates the conference, but the student is responsible for answering parent questions and concerns about his or her learning. Students share what they have learned, show their parents some of their work, and discuss the reasons for their academic progress, grades, and goals.

47. **summative assessment** - The use of some type of assessment to determine the effectiveness of a unit, course of study, or program after it has been completed. An example is a final exam or the test at the end of a unit of study. It should be reliable and generally allows for comparisons among students. It is often used as a means of grading students but may also be used for future planning of curriculum and instruction.

48. **test** - A sample obtained from some systematic procedure that is assumed to have all the characteristics of the whole. Tests are used for gathering data, making comparisons, and recording progress.

49. **validity** - The extent to which a test achieves its purpose and measures what it is supposed to measure.

50. value-added assessment (Growth Model) - A way to analyze test data by reviewing students' test score gains from previous grades and predicting the amount of growth those students are likely to make in a given year. Thus, value-added assessment can show whether particular students have made the expected amount of progress, less progress, or more progress than anticipated. One can look back over several years to measure the long-term impact that a particular teacher or school had on student achievement. Value-added assessment measures growth. Individual students rather than cohorts are traced over time, thus each student serves as his or her own baseline.

Assessment Terminology
Teacher Reflection Page

1. Review the 50 terms defined in this chapter. Categorize them using the chart below.

Very familiar with	Somewhat familiar with	Totally new term to me

2. Identify any terms you feel are misused or misunderstood in your school, school district, state, or by the media. Discuss these with a colleague and make a plan to help others better understand them.

3. What other assessment terms do you hear or use frequently? List them below. If you are not sure what they mean, or if you think they may have different meanings to different people, clarify their meanings.

Chapter 3
Standards and Benchmarks

How do we know what our students need to know?

At the turn of the century, the United States launched a rocket carrying an unmanned vehicle to explore part of the planet Mars. Many of us listened intently to the news hoping to hear about the expected landing and what might be found during this mission. But the vehicle never landed. It was lost in space, they finally admitted, because some of the scientists and engineers were using the metric scale while others had used feet and inches! The measurements were not standardized and the mission ended in failure.

I often travel internationally and am constantly frustrated at the lack of consistency in transportation and telecommunications that would make life easier. Plugs (or "power points" as they are called in some parts of the world) come in a variety of shapes and sizes depending on which country I am in. I have to carry an adapter kit and figure out which plug to use. My cell phone will work in some countries but not in others. In some airports I must take off my shoes, while in other I don't. In some countries I must drive on the right, while in other countries it's the left. There are no worldwide standards, it seems, for transportation, hardware, software, or peripherals.

The 2000 Presidential election was one of the most bizarre and unusual in American history. No doubt this election will be studied for years! Many of the problems were a result of having no national or state standards regarding which votes counted and which did not, no standard method of voting, no standard voting machines, and no standard voter registration procedures. Many of the controversies in this election would not have occurred if known and universally accepted standards were in place.

Ms. Bennett's third graders filed into her classroom on the first day of school. They were an incredibly diverse group in terms of race, ethnicity, experiences, learning styles, readiness, ability levels, talents, parental involvement, and languages spoken. In fact, the only thing "standard'" about them was that they were all in third grade. "How can I ever teach these kids using one set of standards?" Ms. Bennett thought. "And why should I want to? After all, they're individual human beings to be nurtured, not inanimate objects to be put in one mold."

Standards: Why are They Necessary?

Standards play an important role in our everyday lives. From the measurements we use in cooking or travel to the results we get in scientific discoveries or national elections, standards are important and necessary. It makes sense, then, to assume that some standards are needed in the education of American children. The issue is not so much whether we need educational standards but what these standards should be and how they should affect classroom teaching.

First and foremost, educational standards must have broad support among teachers and the general public. This type of ownership is crucial. Because of this, standards have been presented to the public as a whole by addressing two primary concerns:

1. American competitiveness

First is the worry that America is losing its competitiveness. The underlying fear is that if this happens, our economy and our country as a whole will suffer in the long term. Many feel that the way to regain (or retain) top status is to demand more from each child and each school. This concern comes mostly from international studies of achievement in which American students do not typically score near the top. Some think that the way to address this problem is through having educational standards at every level. They believe this can lead to a rigorous and challenging course of study for all students.

Those who are apprehensive about this issue believe that we need to push students to learn more and learn it faster than ever before. They feel that our students can't compete because they are poorly prepared. Ironically, there is little, if any, evidence to support a relationship between economic productivity and high test scores in schools. Nevertheless, this seems to be a persuasive argument for politicians and policy makers to use.

2. Gap in achievement levels

The second concern is the gap between the achievement of high and middle income students as compared to the achievement of lower income and minority students. Part of the thinking behind the standards movement is the desire for this gap to be closed.

One attempt to address the inconsistency in standards between states and the disparity between high and low achieving students was the development of Common Core State Standards. Coordinated by the National Governors Association Center for Best Practices and the Council of Chief State School Officers, they were designed to provide uniformity between the states and lead to higher level thinking for all.

Authentic, standards-based reform has the potential to promote rich, high-level teaching for all students and high levels of support to help all students meet the standards. The reality is that while all students are held to the same standards, all students and all schools don't have equal levels of support or access to the same resources needed to meet these standards. When standards are used to hold students and schools accountable, it seems reasonable that resources such as funding, fully-qualified teachers, and necessary materials and equipment should be equally available to all schools and all teachers. Unfortunately this is sometimes not the case.

Beyond these two concerns is the larger goal of developing an increasing number of students who can function and succeed in a digital-age economy and a global society. In many schools in low socio-economic areas, students are not meeting the standards and are not receiving the quality of education needed for success in our rapidly changing world. In fact, after years of school reform, in spite of our best efforts to raise student achievement, the gap in achievement between white/affluent kids and minority/poor students actually grew. Doing something about this gap is one of the reasons the push for high standards continues.

Benefits of Educational Standards

Developing and implementing high educational standards has many benefits. Such standards:

1. help teachers pay more attention to clear expectations for all students.
2. determine basic concepts and key learnings along with developmentally appropriate levels to attain these learnings.
3. involve teachers and administrators in unpacking the standards so there is ownership at all levels.
4. reflect shared norms and knowledge about what all students should know.
5. break down teacher isolation and call for teacher collaboration around a common set of educational guidelines.
6. have the potential to increase student achievement.
7. provide a consistent way to talk about what is going on in the classroom.
8. establish an excellent list of skills and expectations that can serve as a beginning point for curriculum compacting.
9. provide guidelines for curriculum and teaching to ensure that students will have access to the knowledge needed for their later success.
10. may highlight student performance (or lack thereof) and point the way to improving instruction.
11. give the message that all students need and deserve a high-quality education.
12. change the focus from quantity (such as how many days a child has attended school) to quality (such as what important concepts did that child learn during that time) and results.
13. encourage ongoing high-quality professional development for teachers.
14. can pinpoint problems in the educational achievement of various subgroups within a student population.

Potential Problems with Standards

Standards-based reform also has a number of problems.

1. The sheer number of standards often leads to "drill and kill" content coverage where kids learn loads of facts but little more.

2. Tests on the standards may drive the entire curriculum. "Test prep" has become the defacto curriculum in many schools.

3. Standards often create extra paperwork that becomes more important than teaching and learning.

4. Defining what is important for all students to know is a difficult task when knowledge is increasing and changing so rapidly.

5. In-depth learning and critical/creative thinking often get lost in the push for standards.

6. Some students have already met the age-appropriate benchmarks in skills and knowledge yet must sit through instruction focused on standards they already mastered.

7. Some standards are unrealistic and seem designed to prevent students from passing or graduating.

8. Students who can't meet the standards may become dropouts.

9. Teachers may have no time to explore topics that interest them and their students but are not related to what is tested or listed in the standards.

10. Standards may encourage rote memorization without higher-level thinking.

11. Standards may give some people the impression that all students in a grade begin at the same entry point. This is almost never true.

12. Students are not standardized. It may not be realistic to hold a 14-year-old immigrant child who speaks little English and has never attended school before to the same standards as a native English-speaking middle class student who began preschool at age 3 and has been read to since birth!

13. When standards are not consistent from one state to another, it may seem that students in some states are learning more than those in other states. The reality is that with different standards there is no basis for comparison.

Common Core Standards

One approach in dealing with the fact that standards differ so much between one state and another is the development of Common Core Standards. These standards have come into being as a result of an initiative begun by the states and coordinated by the National Governors Association Center for Best Practices (NGA Center) and the Council of Chief State School Officers (CCSSO). These standards are developed by teachers, postsecondary educators, administrators, and other educational experts with the goal of providing an understandable and coherent framework for educating American children.

Common Core Standards are based on the most effective standards from states throughout the country and from other countries around the world. They provide guidelines about what students throughout the United States are expected to know and be able to do as a result of their schooling. The greatest advantage of such standards is that they are consistent for all students wherever they live. In an age of globalization, and when many students are highly mobile and move from one state to another, such standards seem quite essential.

According to the NGA Center and the CCSSO, these standards:
- Are aligned with college and work expectations
- Are clear, understandable, and consistent
- Include rigorous content and application of knowledge through high-order skills
- Build upon the strengths and the lessons learned through current state standards
- Are informed by other top-performing countries throughout the world
- Are evidence-based

As of this writing, the Common Core Standards are supported by more than 30 states, 2 territories and the District of Columbia. These standards establish appropriate benchmarks for all students and provide a common framework from which each state can be guided to help all students succeed. While these standards establish what students need to learn, they do not dictate what teachers should teach or how they should deliver instruction. While they do not stipulate specific texts, they do require certain critical content for all students.

The Common Core Standards do dictate how the states will implement and use them. Each state will follow its own procedures in adopting and putting them into practice. Additionally, most crucial decisions about what content will be taught is left to the states and local school districts.

Standards and Curriculum

As can be seen from the above lists, educational standards are neither a cure-all nor a disaster. They can be beneficial if we use them in a way that does not cause us to abandon good curriculum design and effective instructional strategies.

A standards-based curriculum can define a challenging course of study and set a minimum level of achievement, proficiency, or competency for all students. Standards are useful when there is a tremendous disparity among teachers of the same subject in terms of how long they spend on a particular topic or skill. Additionally, they can help when there is a great lack of uniformity in what is taught from one classroom to another and little consistency in the knowledge and skills covered in any given course or subject area.

In most school districts, state standards are used as the basis for designing the curriculum. They help us define what should be taught, and then provide the link between what is expected, what is taught, and what is assessed. The essential question of standards is *"What should our students be taught?"* This deals with the fundamentals of curriculum. As important as the questions of *"Who learns what?"* and *"When do they learn it?"* are the questions of *"What new knowledge belongs in the curriculum?"* and *"What content can we eliminate if we include new things?"* Standards furnish us with some guidelines to help answer these questions.

There seems to be three contradictory theories about what students should learn:

1) Give students as much knowledge as possible about as many facts and as many things as possible.

2) Present a few major ideas in depth.

3) Teach process rather than content.

We are facing an information explosion unprecedented in human history. Even if we try to teach as (1) above suggests, in a school year we still can teach only a minute portion of all the knowledge and information that is available. Keeping the status quo with the same list year after year of what students should know and be able to do is not a valid practice in an age of information explosion. The implication is that standards should not be static. They have to constantly be revisited and be revised as knowledge grows and changes.

Usable standards for students in the 21st century should focus on major ideas, skills, and processes. The factual content may change as our knowledge base and views about what it means to be an educated person change. When standards are used in this way, they are valuable tools for educators. At the same time, there are some important guidelines about what we should not do with standards.

We should not:

- create a list of standards at each grade level that is so long it is impossible to pre-test, present, teach, and master.

- make the entire curriculum a list of lower-level skills reflecting minimum standards.

- pace the curriculum so that every standard is covered for every student with no differentiation.

- ignore the learning needs of students who have already met the grade-level standards.

Types of Standards

Standards should be clear to everyone, including teachers, students, and parents. Standards should address only the essentials and not be a laundry list of everything that is to be taught. They should not prescribe teaching methods, devise classroom strategies, or become lesson plans. Standards are the ends, not the means, thus the choice of means should be left to the school or the teacher.

Most experts recommend that standards should be rigorous and world class. Students should be assessed based upon known standards and criteria, not compared to each other. Numerous sets of standards have been developed by each state, educational organizations, and the federal Department of Education.

<u>National Standards</u>

- Have been developed by many different organizations.

- Some are very general while others provide specific benchmarks.

- Basic concepts and key learning components tend to be similar from state to state.

- Standards can be used as guideposts for all educators.

<u>State Standards</u>

- All states have educational standards in most academic subjects.

- Most standards are tied to statewide standardized high-stakes tests.

- Teachers use standards documents to align and drive curriculum and instruction.

<u>Content Standards (What students are expected to know)</u>

- Describe skills and abilities students should have.

- Describe goals for individual students.
- State the knowledge and understandings students are expected to know.
- Often are measured by tests.

Performance Standards (What students are expected to be able to do)

- Emphasize use and application of knowledge.
- Include higher-level thinking skills.
- Are action and problem-solving oriented.
- Can be done at different levels or degrees of competency.
- Are often measured by rubrics.

Benchmarks

Benchmarks are guideposts that identify realistic expectations of how most students should progress through the standards at certain ages and/or grade levels. They are usually developed from a set of standards in some form of a grade level or K-12 continuum. Some type of assessment is usually present to document and monitor progress through the various benchmarks.

Benchmarks can be:

- Specific information and skills to be learned.
- Performance activities or tasks the student should know how to do.

Benchmarks are often more helpful to classroom teachers than the standards themselves because they are tied more directly to grade level and classroom practice.

For Teacher Reflection

Which standards and benchmarks am I most familiar with?

How have I used standards as guidelines in my teaching?

How have they improved the day-to-day instruction in my classroom?

In what ways have they been detrimental to my students or my teaching?

What is the difference between teaching to the standards and teaching to the test?

Standards and Assessment

Standards imply standards assessment. However, there are many questions surrounding the issue of standards and how to assess them.

- Precisely which standards should be tested?
- Should standards reflect facts or concepts.
- What assessments will be used to determine whether students are reaching the standards?
- Must standards always be assessed using standardized tests or can they be assessed in other ways?

These and similar questions make this a very complex problem and concern.

Standards-based reform is about setting higher standards and measuring the attainment of those standards in criterion-referenced ways. As students progress through the school system, the standards for performance rise steadily, and accountability is directly tied to these standards. With standards, everyone knows what is expected and no allowances are made for substandard performance.

The public looks to tests as a way of measuring how well students have met the standards. If standards and accountability are to improve schools and help children learn rather than punish teachers, schools, and students, we must ensure that 1) the standards are appropriate, 2) ways to assess standards are valid, relevant, fair and unbiased, and 3) implementation of standards and testing is reasonable. High standards and high-stakes testing are not necessarily the same thing, though many perceive that they are.

Good standards-based assessment is not always a test. It is not always paper/pencil and is not always from the book. Other alternate forms of assessment to use to determine achievement of the standards include:

- Interviews
- Open-ended questions
- Student explanations of why and how
- Real life problem solving
- Rubrics
- Student activities tied to the standards
- Standards-based report cards

All students may not meet a given standard but many may be working toward it. We need to document where they are and what they still need to do to meet the standard. Response to Intervention (RTI) is an approach that helps teachers monitor individual student progress toward a standard.

One intention of requiring mandatory standards is to make lazy teachers and students change their ways. From this viewpoint, the source of failure may be seen as the student's lack of motivation to take tough courses and work hard in school. The remedy often becomes a demand that students achieve the standards — or else! Sometimes this strategy backfires. Teachers in low performing schools drill students on the standards, teach to the standards (or to the test), and practice test-taking skills. The results are mixed. Some students make great progress. But in spite of all our efforts, others seem to fall further behind. Implementing NCLB with teacher pay tied to student mastery of the standards may motivate some but can also harm others. However, another approach showing some promise leading to mastery of the standards is the value-added/growth model.

Meanwhile, many high-performing schools have geared up to meet the standards, piling on more homework than ever and teaching difficult subjects and courses at earlier grade levels than they did a generation ago. Students in these schools have an abundance of homework, take tough courses, and get into the best colleges in the world. These students probably didn't need higher standards in the first place! By contrast, students in poor urban or rural schools who have to meet equivalent standards often drop out or fail the high-stakes tests.

Motivation is more complex than telling students they must pass a high-stakes exam or be retained. High quality instruction, the energy and enthusiasm of good teachers, and individualized support are all needed to help struggling students reach the higher standards. When current test scores are the focus, motivation to meet the standards fades. These test scores usually don't help show individual student growth toward mastering the standards. Yet one strategy to motivate struggling students might be to show them how much progress they have made toward the final goal. The RTI approach used in many schools is one avenue we can take in this direction.

We need to use standards and the assessment of those standards more as a motivator and less as a punishment. Fallout from low scores can wear out well-meaning teachers and administrators. Harsh sanctions aimed at students, teachers, and schools who don't meet the standards are not the best or most educationally sound approach. We need to find ways to improve schools, not punish them. Standards should be used to help each child improve, not to punish those who cannot possibly bridge the gap between where they are educationally and where they are supposed to be according to tough standards and benchmarks.

Using Data to Drive Instruction

Data is information about a student, his or her work, test scores, learning preferences, readiness levels, work habits, and family involvement. It is often organized for analysis and used to make decisions.

Schools usually have huge amounts of data about their students including:

- Standardized test scores
- Teacher-made exams/quizzes
- Pre-test scores
- Rubrics from activities/assignments
- Teacher observations
- Student portfolios
- Attendance records
- Conference logs
- Surveys or questionnaires

However, just having data is not helpful in driving instruction. Instead, it is necessary to organize the data so that it makes sense and points the way to instructional change. Then data is helpful because it is easier to analyze and understand. When this happens, you can use data to monitor student progress, plan instructional interventions, and see results.

Base your instructional decisions on the most up-to-date, accurate, and easily understood data. Promote student achievement by using the data to show you what the student's needs are. Then consider research-based interventions or strategies you could use to help that student achieve.

The amount of data is not as important as how the data is used. Schools can be overrun by too much data that is never used by anyone to monitor student progress, make instructional decisions, or bring about positive change.

Before using your data to make a decision or to drive instructional change, ask yourself these questions:

- What does the data reveal?
- Is it reliable?
- How many different types of data did I collect?
- Does different data tell me the same thing?
- What changes in instruction seem logical based on this data?
- How will I collect new data during the change process?
- How will I monitor student progress using this data?

Assisting Students Who Do Not Meet the Standards

Not every student enters school with the same background experiences and abilities. There is some concern that having higher standards and having universal standards may be contradictory educational goals, and doubts about all students meeting the highest standards are widespread. It seems obvious that provisions should be made to assist students in meeting the standards. As educators we need to ask ourselves how we can best help students who have difficulty accomplishing this task. What assistance will students who fail to reach the standards receive, and how will schools prepare teachers to teach them?

Standards do not have to be tied to age and grade level, but in most American schools they are. In meeting the standards, we must allow for the fact that students are at different starting points and learn in different ways. Many children need more time to master basic skills that lead to mastery of the standards and benchmarks.

There are a number of pro-active strategies we can use to help all students meet the standards:

- Giving individual attention and extra help
- Teaching these students in different ways (for example, using differing modalities or the multiple intelligences in curriculum planning)
- Providing more time to meet the standards
- Offering remediation, including prevention and intervention

- Analyzing assessment results, determining strengths and weaknesses, and designing instruction accordingly, linking it to academic standards
- Aligning curriculum to the standards
- Providing teacher training to support using standards and assessment to improve instruction
- Using resources that are based on benchmarked content standards
- Using the RTI approach with targeted students to see progress toward a goal

Standards and Creative Teaching

Creative teaching should be the goal in every school. At the same time, meeting specific benchmarks and standards is also necessary. These two goals do not need to contradict one another. Engaging kids creatively may bring a better mastery of the standards than "drill and kill" activities do.

Learning facts is not inherently bad or uncreative! Actually, understanding a subject begins with building a knowledge base, including factual information. Learning the facts by using them to think critically and creatively may be one of the best strategies for meeting the standards. This allows students to successfully engage in inquiry-based learning when they use the facts to discover their own strategies for solving problems.

Standards sometimes make teachers rely on a schedule of instruction to make sure they cover all the standards rather than pacing instruction to meet individual student needs. Standards usually establish a minimum level of learning, but often this minimum becomes the maximum. Students who have already mastered the information are forced to go over it again and again instead of learning new material or creatively exploring other topics of interest that are not included in the standards.

In a creativity-oriented standards-based classroom, inventive and creative strategies should be encouraged. Conceptual understanding and higher-level thinking should be valued more than memorization of facts. Students should learn that there are often multiple ways to solve the same problem and should be inspired to create their own strategies when problem solving. Instructional activities should encourage creative communication, with thought-provoking questions, speculations, and investigations as the norm.

In an ideal world educational standards might not be necessary. If every child had a gifted teacher who could individualize and teach to every learning style, all students would finish school completely competent. But we live and teach in a less than perfect world. Because of this, it is helpful not to look at the ideal, but rather to look at best practices. The following list will help you formulate practical ideas about implementing standards.

Best Practices for Implementing Standards

1. Meet in small groups to unpack the standards, review them in light of current curriculum, and put them in a format such as a curriculum map that will be helpful for ongoing planning of curriculum and instruction.

2. Look at test scores and other data about student achievement to see areas in which students are strong and areas that need more work.

3. Translate the standards into clear and doable instructional goals and objectives.

4. Align your curriculum to the standards in such a way that you focus on key concepts and ideas.

5. Develop or revise instructional units based on groups of standards. Earmark priority instructional units or topics. Borrow units other districts have developed that meet your priorities.

6. Use district-level or school-based resource personnel or outside consultants to help find and/or develop high-level instructional materials.

7. Find ways to integrate social studies, science, math, language arts, technology, and other subject areas.

8. Use learning theories such as learning modalities, learning styles, brain compatible learning, and multiple intelligences as tools to help you assist all students in meeting the standards. (See *Teaching Tools for the 21st Century* by Carolyn Coil, Pieces of Learning, Marion, Illinois, for more information.)

9. Give professional feedback to others and seek it for your own teaching. Analyze your own effectiveness, and use the feedback to continuously improve your own instructional practice.

10. Focus on what the students need to know and need to be able to do to meet the standards. Then brainstorm ways to help them do these things.

11. Examine student work with other teachers and come to consensus about criteria for quality work and the meaning of grades.

12. Encourage students to be active, self-directed learners who can construct their own knowledge bases.

13. Engage students in self-assessment, teach them ways to look at their own learning, and have them share the responsibility for learning.

14. Allow students to work in groups frequently, sharing knowledge and learning to problem solve together.

15. Become more of a facilitator and less of an information giver.

16. Use standards-based report cards as a way to show student progress.

Using Standards to Integrate Curriculum, Instruction, and Assessment

Standards provide us with guidelines for examining and integrating curriculum, instruction, and assessment. Below are recommended strategies to implement in your classroom.

1. Integration of standards from two or more subject areas
2. Cooperative learning and flexible grouping
3. Active communication between students
4. Innovative questioning techniques
5. Project/product-based learning
6. Teacher as facilitator
7. Problem solving
8. Integration of technology
9. Reflective thinking (metacognition)
10. Student responsibility for learning

For Teacher Reflection

1. Which of the 16 Best Practices seem feasible for my school and situation? Share this list with other teachers in your grade level, teaching team, or department. Together design an implementation plan based on the Best Practices and other ideas you may have.

2. Look at the list of 10 strategies to implement in your classroom. Brainstorm practical ways you could accomplish some of these ideas in your classroom.

Chapter 4
Standardized Tests

The Good, The Bad and The Ugly!

> *I do not spend an inordinate amount of time preparing my students for standardized tests. I do use our curriculum alignment to make sure I am covering the standards and skills that are necessary for them to know at test time. I do some timed math computation to give them experience with this type of testing. I feel if I do the best job I can do in my classroom, for the most part my students will be successful on the tests. — 2nd grade teacher*

Why the Emphasis on Testing?

Accountability is a part of life in most of today's jobs and professional endeavors. Thus, it should not be surprising that it is emphasized in education as well. The teacher quoted above seems quite comfortable with her abilities as a teacher and her students' abilities to succeed on the tests. Other teachers I interviewed were not nearly as relaxed about the issue of standardized testing.

This emphasis on test taking definitely increases pressure on schools and teachers. Norm-referenced tests seek to sort and rank students. This results in teachers being concerned about how they will look if their children do poorly. Many principals, especially those in low-performing schools, worry about their own jobs.

Pressure about testing can create tension in high-performing schools as well. When students score at the 99-98 percentile on standardized tests, it is impossible for teachers to meet the district goal of improving test scores by 5 points the following year! Yet this is what some teachers are being asked to do. Additionally, many generally high-performing schools may have one or two subgroups of students who perform poorly.

High-stakes testing does make us pay attention to all students, especially those who might otherwise do poorly and fall between the cracks. Test results can serve a variety of diagnostic functions that may well be their most important use in terms of instruction. When tests are used as diagnostic tools, they help us determine specific strengths and weaknesses in individual students and in our teaching.

Educational accountability generally consists of looking at average scores for an entire school on national or state tests. Testing can also give us reliable long-term data about a particular student or sub-group of students.

It seems evident that accountability using test scores as the sole criterion for success often fails to take into account differences among students and schools. A teacher must work with the students and families he or she is given. A teacher in a school with an upper middle class student population can easily look fine if judged by standardized tests, because these students will usually do well. On the other hand, that same teacher may not look nearly as good in a school with a different student population.

The Every Student Succeeds Act requires annual standardized testing in grades 3-8 and once in high school. Districts often add their own diagnostic and practice tests. Therefore, politicians and school officials have come to think that test scores are the most important thing (or the only important thing) in assessing at student learning. Educational accountability should be about more than test scores. However, nearly universally, students' test scores are used by top administrators to hold principals accountable and are sometimes used in decisions about teacher pay, hiring, firing, promotion, and transfer.

Sometimes teachers cover the standards that will be tested while leaving out worthwhile objectives or information which is tested. The result of gearing instruction only toward the test is that it may produce a very narrow curriculum and hamper flexibility and creativity in both teachers and students.

Uses of Standardized Test Scores

In spite of the fact that American students are among the most tested in the world, we rarely use test results to help us produce better and more able students. Most often test scores are used to sort and select students or to punish students, teachers, schools, and/or school districts. In some districts, teacher pay is tied to students' test scores.

Standardized test scores are often used to rank schools and teachers. In some cases, parents use test results to determine the qualifications of a teacher. This seems unfair. In fact, if a standardized test is the only measurement that holds teachers accountable, then the American educational system is in jeopardy. A teacher, like each and every student, is so much more than a standardized test!

At best, standardized test scores (as well as many other types of assessments) should have a variety of uses. Besides determining eligibility for funding, they may:

1. be used as diagnostic tools.
2. provide data for setting educational goals.
3. serve as a guide in planning for improvement by helping teachers evaluate programs, curriculum, and instruction.
4. be a means to compare and rank schools and students.

Diagnostic Tools

Tests can be used as diagnostic tools as teachers plan for remediation or to help a teacher, school, or grade level to look at how they are teaching targeted skills, standards, or certain aspects of the curriculum. It should be a guide to show teachers what they are doing right, what they need to change, and what works best for students. When tests are used in this fashion, they can help teachers in planning differentiated classroom instruction and in forming flexible groups for learning.

Provide Data

Standardized tests are used because they provide data and a results orientation that are essential to improvement. Test results provide educators with a common instructional focus. They also encourage teachers to abandon ineffective practices.

Planning Improvement

Educators need to look at test scores to determine if a student has improved or regressed in performance. They need to use tests to determine whether their instruction was effective, to find out what their students have learned, and to identify which students need additional help. Test results can help guide students and show them how to take what they have learned and use it in a variety of ways. This approach is called the value-added or growth model.

Students can use tests to see if their study skills are paying off. The structure provided by tests may be limiting, but many students need some structure in order to learn, and many teachers need this structure in order to plan effective curriculum and instruction. Test scores help both teachers and students target steps for improvement.

Basis for Comparison

When test results are used as a basis for comparison, students are compared to others who have taken the same test. This may be those in the same class, the same grade, the same grade the year before, the same school, the same school district, or students all across the nation. One problem in using tests for comparison is that we often end up comparing "apples and oranges." It doesn't work to look at test scores for a grade level one year and plan for next year's students based on those scores. Next year's class will have entirely different students with different strengths, weaknesses, learning styles, problems, and home situations.

Many people believe that administering more and harder tests will pave the way to better, more effective schools. This would have us believe that a successful school is always one that enrolls large numbers of students who pass the standardized tests. The problem schools, then, are those that enroll the greatest percentage of students who fail. Unfortunately, looking at test scores in this way takes no note of home, environmental, or socioeconomic factors which may affect how students test.

Educators often respond to the pressure for good test scores in two ways. Some try test prep curriculum designed to raise test scores. Others try a range of instructional strategies that do not focus so much on test scores as they do on increasing the number of students who can function productively and meet the challenges of the 21st century.

Higher test scores and reaching higher levels of learning are not necessarily the same thing. Some students say that real learning is being shoved aside to raise test scores. For example, students often learn to write essays using only the boilerplate format favored by test scorers.

One problem with computer-scored assessments is that they do not take into account the test taker's thought process. They do not fully measure students' critical and inventive powers. Yet tests should be reflections of how students are thinking. Tests are much more valuable when students can show why they were thinking a certain way and then are allowed to go back and revise or correct the mistakes they made. When this happens, testing becomes an excellent instructional tool.

Helping Students Become Good Test Takers

Standardized high-stakes tests help to decide issues such as grade placement, retention, college admissions, graduate school admissions, special education placement, and admission to special programs as well as to diagnose strengths and weaknesses. Yet these tests do not tell the whole story. Many students who are not totally successful on tests are still very successful as students.

However, until we as a nation move away from the heavy emphasis currently placed on standardized testing, perhaps we have no choice but to teach our students how to be good test takers. We want them to maximize their ability to transpose their knowledge and skills on a test. If they do not understand the techniques they need to use to maximize this transfer, students will underperform and not do as well as they should on tests.

Specific strategies to teach test-taking skills:

- Send home practice packets to prepare for the test.
- Explain the format of the test.
- Set up classroom assessments in the same format as the test.
- Give practice tests.
- Practice listening skills all year.
- Teach the content of the test.
- Give practice sessions, and do daily activities which use the skills tested.
- Show students how to use the process of elimination.
- Practice completing the easier questions first.
- Give the same amount of time to complete a classroom assignment as the time allowed to complete a portion of the test.
- Point out key words and phrases in test questions.
- Teach how to read for details, listen, and follow directions.
- Ask students to repeat the directions back to you.
- Teach students to think in a logical and problem solving manner.
- Do problems of the day to increase abilities in problem solving and mental math.

Students not only need to practice test taking, they also need to develop strategies to avoid being stressed and anxious during the testing period. Help by giving them opportunities to gain confidence as test takers. Giving them lots of positive feedback is a beginning step in building self confidence. Because they need to believe they are capable of answering correctly, self-confidence is important. Presenting skills and concepts in a way that requires higher-order thinking will help students feel confident about their abilities to solve the simpler problems presented on the test.

Teachers are often told to help their students relax during the testing period and to work on ways to calm students during testing situations when there is a lot of anxiety. This seems a rather difficult task in a media-hyped testing environment. A special section about school testing was part of a recent edition of a local newspaper. Twelve full pages were devoted to describing the importance of the high-stakes tests in one local school district within the region. The test environment is described as follows:

> *On the days students are scheduled to take the exam, they won't be allowed to bring textbooks, scrap paper, or back packs to their classrooms. They'll also be prohibited from carrying anything out of the classroom after they finish their tests. Finally, students will be under constant supervision by proctors — not their classroom teachers — while the test is being administered.*

It seems it would be almost impossible for anyone, students or teachers, to relax in such a punitive environment. Why would anyone think this is good for student learning or a good environment to find out what students know and can do?

One area of test taking in which students generally need practice is in developing the ability to work rapidly enough to finish the timed portion of the test. Students need practice in order to learn how to budget their time to complete all the questions. They also need help in proofreading and in learning how to go back to completed test questions to verify their answers. Some students have problems with looking at all choices before making a decision. They learn early that tests are based on time, so they choose the first answer they read that looks like it might be correct.

Teachers should spend time building all of these test-taking skills, but this should not be the entire curriculum. Especially important is not to keep endlessly drilling and drilling students who already know the answers and are comfortable with the test format.

Time Spent in Testing and Test Preparation

> *Students hate these tests. The tests are too long. No matter what we do, they produce too much anxiety because parents and the outside world place so much importance on them. We are a nation who wants to assess, test, and evaluate everything because the general public seems to think that is the way to make education better. — 6th grade teacher*
>
> *My students will have 13 days of standardized testing between January and March. They get so tired of it! I dislike it most of all when I think about all of the instructional time that is lost in test practice and test taking. — 8th grade teacher*

One problem in using standardized tests as such an important measure of learning is that teachers spend too much time in test preparation, and too much focus is sometimes put on test scores. They are not really able to "teach." They are too busy making sure their test scores are acceptable. We certainly need to periodically check students' learning, but we don't need to inundate students with tests. Even the most successful students can be drowned by tests and get lost in them.

Sometimes students just get tired of all the test taking, including taking the practice tests. The result is that they may not bother to do their best because of test burnout.

Too much time spent in preparation for testing can limit a student's comprehensive education. It can drain the energy, excitement, and life from any classroom. Instead of test preparation, teachers should be spending most of their time creating an environment in which students are excited about learning. If we can sustain this enthusiasm for learning throughout the school years, we will create lifelong learners.

As discussed, one of our goals needs to be to encourage students to be good test takers because tests will be around for a long time, and students should be prepared for them. However, there should be other ways to assess achievement besides standardized tests. We shouldn't be spending most of the school year preparing students for tests.

Test Prep
Teacher Reflection Page

1. Do test-prep curricula help students learn broad content and skills, get higher test scores, or both? What are the advantages and disadvantages of this type of curriculum?

2. What long term benefits, if any, do you see in test practice or in having students take sample tests before they take the "real thing?"

3. What strategies do you think are most effective in helping students do well on high-stakes tests?

4. In your experience, does test preparation take too much time away from other types of instruction?

5. What are your best strategies for helping students do well on other tests?

Reproducible

Connections Between What is Taught and Test Content

> *The pressure to raise test scores may ultimately lower the quality of education after teachers, feeling the pressure, limit their teaching to the skills and content tested. — 3rd grade teacher*
>
> *Not all of the material that needs to be taught is covered on the high-stakes standardized test. For example, if only mammals and insects are covered in the science portion, does that mean that we don't teach the children about other types of animals? That would seem to be nonsense, but that is how many teachers are now teaching. If it isn't written down as a standard to be tested, it isn't considered important to teach it. — 1st grade teacher*

In many school districts across our country, the entire curriculum is aligned to standardized tests. However, just because a test is standardized to national or local norms, it does not mean that it is based on state or national standards. When there is a true alignment of the curriculum with a standards-based, standardized test, this is beneficial as the standards are more likely to be taught and learned. Even so, it is not beneficial to students when teachers simply teach to the test.

Aligning curriculum and instruction to a standards-based standardized test can help teachers pace their instruction. It helps them make sure they teach the areas that the test covers. It also focuses their attention on important material that may not be covered in the curriculum or textbook. However, as any test only reflects a *sampling* of what students have learned, it should serve merely as a guideline for planning and teaching. A *test sample* is only a portion of what needs to be learned and should never be looked upon as the *whole*. Unfortunately, we often look at test scores as the only thing that is important.

Testing and Federal Laws and Mandates

No Child Left Behind (2002-2015) created an enormous amount of pressure on schools to raise test scores. The proliferation in standardized testing that occurred during those years increasingly met with resistance from many parents. Due to the expanded testing burden on their children, some parents called for fewer or no tests and a lesser role for the federal government in education. Teachers, too, disliked the "one-size-fits-all model of test, blame and punish."

Because of the increased emphasis on testing, schools have focused their emphasis on test mastery and test preparation. A school's test scores or even an individual teacher's test scores come with a component of accountability. In some states, teachers receive merit pay if their students have high test scores. In other places, entire school faculties have been fired due to the low test scores of the school's students.

Therefore, test scores have a powerful influence on what occurs in the classroom. Tests often shape school goals and dominate instruction. The news media often compares the test scores of different schools, and this leads to the labeling of schools. Thus, one school may be known as a School of Excellence while another is a Failing School. Because of this, teachers spend a great deal of instructional time getting ready for the tests.

What standardized test scores don't usually show is individual student progress. Most of the time, the scores of this year's class are compared to the scores of last year's class. On the other hand, a value-added or growth model measures how much an individual student's test scores have improved over time. It can show if the student has made the expected amount of progress, less than expected, or more than expected. Some districts and schools are using the value-added or growth model to assess student progress. This approach has a great deal of potential and gets away from the one-size-fits-all model of grade-level standardized testing.

Teaching only tested standards carries with it the risk of not expanding students' knowledge beyond the basics. When curriculum is totally aligned to the test, important knowledge and skills not on the test may not be taught. In many school districts, elementary students are tested only in reading and math. An outcome is that science and social studies are being almost totally ignored. Does this mean that science and social studies are no longer important for elementary students to know?

If teachers just teach to the test, students' individual needs, learning styles, and creativity aren't addressed. When teachers try to teach only the objectives on the test, they do not enrich or expand the curriculum. Teachable moments are often lost due to these factors. A stressful environment can be the result, and students are the losers.

Kyung Hee Kim from the College of William and Mary in Virginia recently analyzed nearly 300,000 scores from the Torrance Test of Creative Thinking, a test that has long been considered the preeminent instrument for assessing creativity. He found that creativity scores in America had steadily been rising until 1990. Since that time, however, creativity scores have been falling significantly. Additionally, he notes that the greatest decline is in the scores of children in grades K-6. (*Newsweek*, July 10, 2010)

My conclusion from examining this research as well as from personal observation and anecdotal evidence from teachers is that today's students are less creative than those from earlier generations. Perhaps a reason for this is that the pressure to get through the curriculum leaves less time for creative endeavors. This could cause an additional problem. Will first-rate teachers who view effective teaching as a creative art more than test preparation begin to feel limited, stifled, and discouraged in a field they once felt was exciting and energizing? Will these teachers leave teaching and take with them the creative spark so necessary for superb teaching and student motivation? Only time will tell.

Clearly, standardized testing is a mixed bag. Certainly there are beneficial aspects to this type of testing. There are also harmful effects for students and for teachers. Both points of view are summarized on the next four pages.

Beneficial Aspects of Standardized Tests

1. High-stakes testing draws more attention to the state standards and curriculum. If a teacher teaches to the test, he or she is most likely teaching the grade-level standards.

2. Tests establish and assess respectable standards for literacy and numeracy and give schools focus in improving and refining instructional practices particularly in reading, writing, and math.

3. Tests and the standards that are tested can be used to help plan curriculum to best meet the needs of students.

4. Tests expose students to material that may be used to determine their academic futures.

5. Students who take standardized tests are more likely to be exposed to what others are learning across the country. It may give them a more global perspective.

6. Tests usually lead to greater standardization across schools in terms of what is taught and when.

7. Tests clarify what students are expected to learn. Test scores form objective criteria and minimum standards for student learning. They can provide numerical and intelligible data about both performance and improvement.

8. Testing emphasizes the need to bring all students to a minimum proficiency level.

9. Testing provides the means to show mastery of specific skills.

10. Testing makes students realize that they are accountable for the information that is taught in class. It provides a measure to show them what they have learned.

11. Tests can help teachers diagnose individual strengths and weaknesses so they can remediate and direct students in a more individual manner.

12. Students can use test scores to see their own strengths and weaknesses and to set goals for improvement.

13. Test scores can give vital information about patterns of strengths and weaknesses in a classroom, school, or district.

14. Test scores may give us an unbiased comparison of student achievement that can be used to show growth and progress from year to year and as a diagnostic tool for future learning and educational programming.

15. When students do well or improve in an area, test scores can be very encouraging because they show improvement in an objective way. If they understand the scale and know what the numbers mean, it is a solid way for them to look at their own educational accomplishments.

16. Testing may encourage students to achieve goals and have a strong work ethic. Students are proud when they score well.

17. Accountability measured by test scores may give both teachers and students higher expectations for student performance.

18. Test scores can lead to more support and help for low-performing students and schools.

19. Developing test-taking skills can help students learn to read for details, think logically, and devise strategies for problem solving.

20. If the test incorporates higher-level thinking skills, it may encourage teachers to include problem solving and critical thinking in their curriculum and daily lessons.

Harmful Aspects of Standardized Tests

1. Too much emphasis on testing can make the entire curriculum disjointed.

2. There is a minimum of time to incorporate hands-on problem solving and student projects. In-depth study, extension, and enrichment activities are lost when the focus is teaching to the test.

3. Many tests do not promote creative and critical thinking. Testing limits teacher creativity and teachers may lose the joy of teaching. Students' creative thinking may also be lost because of time constraints and the rigidity of test-driven curriculum.

4. It is more difficult to infuse individual student interests into the curriculum, and thus many times student motivation is lost because of this.

5. Students are not given opportunities to discover their own strengths and develop them.

6. Subjects and topics not tested may be neglected or totally eliminated from the curriculum.

7. Too much pressure is placed on teachers to cover the skills in a set time and for all students to learn within a set time frame. Individual differences and differentiated curriculum may not be considered.

8. When test review and practice take most of the classroom time, it is difficult to provide ample time for student-directed learning.

9. Standardized tests do not allow teachers to look at the whole child. Assessment should include test results, daily classroom performance, projects and products, and report card grades.

10. Some students are not good test takers. Students may suffer from test anxiety and have problems with the time allowed for many tests.

11. Many items on the test may be covered in the curriculum but are tested in such a way that the students get frustrated, don't show what they actually know, and don't score as well as they should.

12. Standardized tests rarely allow for ambiguity, different perspectives, or the fact that many thought-provoking questions do not have a right and a wrong answer. Tests make students become convergent thinkers who are always looking for the one right answer. Real life does not work that way!

13. Students are not being taught to think globally and see the big picture. They are being taught to be successful on tests.

14. Standardized tests give unfair comparisons of schools and teachers. Most tests are not designed to give credit for the amount of effort a teacher gives at a low performing school. There is little or no consideration of outside factors. If the test scores are low, the teacher is blamed and is looked upon as a poor teacher.

15. There may be a lack of sensitivity to minority or ethnic groups resulting in bias on the tests.

16. Measuring something does not create change. Tests are useless unless results cause curriculum and instruction revision and individualization for some students.

17. Teachers may overuse instructional materials that mimic state test items. Often this leads to a boring and lower-level curriculum.

18. There may be a reduction of the pool of tested students if they do not show up on testing days or if they do not take certain courses.

19. The arts and programs for gifted students have been eliminated in many schools because bringing all students to a minimum level in the tested standards is all that matters to many school boards and school district leaders.

20. School should be challenging and motivating. Learning should be a privilege and a joy. Tests are none of these.

Standardized Testing
Teacher Reflection Page

With a colleague or colleagues, discuss the questions and concerns below.

1. There are a number of positive aspects to standardized testing and a number of negative aspects. In the space below, list the most significant aspects for you.

Positive	Negative

2. How has standardized testing affected your teaching on a day-to-day basis?

3. If a certain topic or skill is not included in the standardized test, do you think it is important to teach it? Why or why not?

4. What are the best strategies you have used to lessen test anxiety and stress in your students?

5. What are the best strategies you have used to emphasize the importance of these tests to your students?

Chapter 5
Traditional Assessment/Alternative Assessment

Would You Like Regular or Diet?

I am a big advocate for alternative assessment. I helped our school write a proposal to end testing of our first graders and use portfolio assessment instead. This worked so much better for our student population. Parents support it once it is explained to them and they understand its value. — 1st grade teacher

Traditional testing is one of those necessities of education. It makes the students take their work more seriously. They know there is a consequence for not doing what is required. It helps the teacher and the class stay focused and doesn't allow us to come up with excuses about why some students can't successfully do the work. — 6th grade teacher

One of the biggest areas of concern, discussion, and controversy in education today is the assessment of student learning. Many educators advocate alternative assessment while others feel student progress is more easily and more reliably measured using traditional tests and other assessments with definitive correct and incorrect answers. There appears to be no consensus as to whether traditional or alternative assessments are best in terms of student learning.

The public often looks upon traditional assessment such as standardized testing as the best way to measure student progress. As a culture, we seem to have an ingrained inclination favoring elements that can be measured and counted. But simply looking at scores and putting numbers on everything students do is not enough. There are many other factors involved in the day-to-day educational process that are almost impossible to measure. Kids are not *things*. We cannot measure them as accurately as we would an inanimate object such as a glass of water or the width of railroad tracks.

In this chapter we will:

- Look at the components of good assessment strategies.
- Identify the advantages and disadvantages of alternative and traditional assessment measures.
- Examine methods to design alternative assessment tasks.

It is extremely difficult to construct and score an excellent assessment instrument. No matter whether it is a traditional assessment such as an objective test or an alternative assessment such as a rubric for a student project, most of the assessments we use in the classroom are good but are far from perfect.

Following are characteristics of both types of assessments. Most teachers will use a mix of traditional and alternative assessments in the course of a school year. We want to make sure we are using both types wisely and well.

Elements of Alternative Assessments

Below are eight characteristics of top quality alternative assessments. Use this list as a checklist as you inspect the assessment instruments you use. This list provides you with guidelines to use as you design and choose assessments for your students.

_____ 1. **Meaningful**

Assessment is best when it has value beyond itself. In other words, it should be meaningful and have application in other areas of learning and/or life. Assessment should reflect what students know about content outcomes and standards. The results should be used to improve student performance and knowledge. For example, pre-tests and other forms of assessment should be used by teachers to develop curriculum, individualize instruction as necessary, prepare for upcoming lessons, and decide on varied teaching strategies.

_____ 2. **Open-ended**

Assessment works best when students use higher levels of thinking to develop their own responses to questions, topics, and issues. When this happens, assessment is tailored to the needs, strengths, and weaknesses of the learner. Learning logs, anecdotal records, portfolios, performance-based tasks, essays, journal entries, open-ended questions, discussions, peer response sessions, and interviews are forms of assessment that allow for an open student response.

_____ 3. **Realistic**

Students tend to have a very realistic focus toward learning. Many students ask, "Why do I need to do this? Why do I need to know that?" When the only answer a teacher can give is, "Because it's on the test," that's a sign the assignment and the assessment are not very beneficial to student learning in the long term. Just learning the information for a test doesn't mean students can apply what they know. Application and analysis should be part of student assessment, not simply the rote memorization of facts.

_____ 4. **Useful outside the classroom**

The best assessments show us if a student knows how to solve problems and think critically. They indicate to what extent students are able to use ideas, theories, methods, concepts, or principles in situations encountered in daily life. Worthwhile products and performances generally apply in real life settings and connect to the world outside the classroom. These types of assessments let us know how well students can use what they have learned, not just how well they can memorize and put something on paper.

_____ 5. **Variety**

Good assessments provide a number of different ways to evaluate student learning. Teachers should not assess everything the same way because all students do not learn in the same way. The ideal is to have a variety of different learning tasks to assess the same skills and knowledge. Projects that offer multiple approaches to the same content are often good ways to assess student learning, especially when the students can have choices in selecting the project and give input as to how they would like their work to be assessed.

_____ 6. **Interdisciplinary**
Quality assessment tasks are interdisciplinary and include a number of different subjects or skills within the same learning activity. Such assessments integrate a variety of content areas, skills, and knowledge effectively and creatively. This helps teachers cover a number of standards and benchmarks within the same activity and helps students see the connections between different subjects and concepts.

_____ 7. **Standard criteria**
Valid assessments base scoring on a set of specific standard criteria. Fairness is an important concern when one considers scoring alternative assessment tasks. Such assessments should have consistency in expectations, criteria, and scoring. This plays an important role in the diagnosis of specific strengths and weaknesses in individual students, a class, or school. The criteria should reflect the learning outcomes and standards addressed.

_____ 8. **Specific objectives**
Effective assessments are based on defined criteria and a set of outcomes that are established before the task is started. All those who meet the standards and demonstrate the desired outcomes can be said to have successfully completed the assessment task. When assessment is based on specific teaching objectives, there is a link between assessment and instruction.

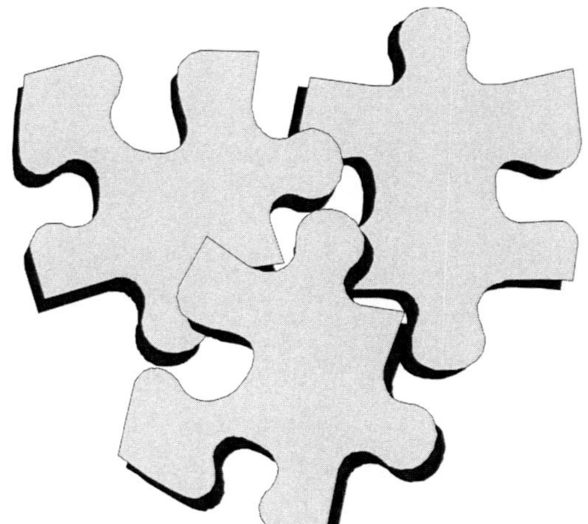

A View of Traditional Assessments

What should be the role of tests and quizzes in assessment? Many teachers believe their students would never be motivated to do any work unless they knew there would be a test on the material at some point. This seems to be a reasonable point of view. However, what most teachers don't realize is that traditional tests and quizzes generally motivate only the better students because they are the ones who enjoy seeing good scores as concrete results of their work and their abilities. These tests do not usually motivate struggling students who often have an attitude of failure and resignation before they begin and figure, "Why bother?"

Well-constructed tests and quizzes help teachers target essential skills and concepts that must be taught and provide a way to document that they have been mastered. Test scores can encourage students when they see their progress in learning the required material.

On the other hand, standardized tests and other forms of traditional assessment may project a feeling of elitism on the part of students who do well. Students and parents like this feeling, but only if the test results are high! Individual, class, or school test score rankings never motivate those at the bottom of the list.

Unfortunately, traditional assessments are used more and more for purposes beyond those for which they were intended. Test results and honor roll lists are routinely published in local newspapers, on the Internet, and in various reports. Students and schools compete with one another and are compared to one another based on test scores. Stakes are so high that some educators have resorted to cheating to make their test results more favorable. Administrators and teachers may lose their jobs based on low test scores or get merit pay based on high scores. Realtors even use these results to sell homes in certain geographic locations.

During any school year, assessments given to students are generally a mix of traditional and alternative forms. There are definite pluses and minuses to both types. The following charts give detailed information about the advantages and disadvantages of each.

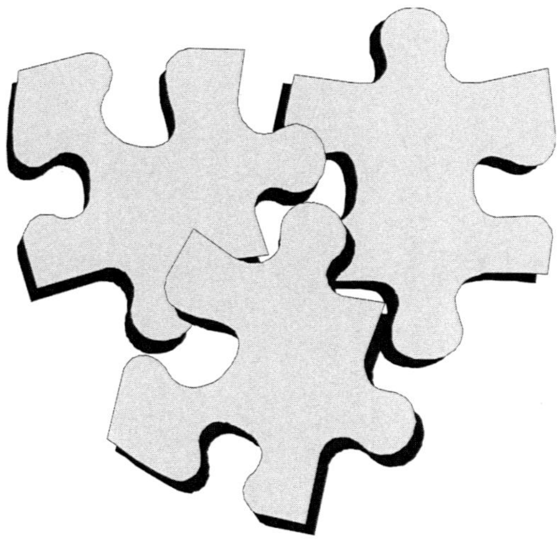

Traditional Assessment

Characteristic	Advantages	Disadvantages
Purpose is accountability.	Teachers will make sure certain content is taught. Shows how students compare to one another. All students are required to master certain standards.	Not enough emphasis on long term outcomes. Teachers may be held accountable for variables out of their control. Focus on bringing all students to minimum standards rather than to maximum accomplishment. Doesn't always focus on individual growth and improvement.
Objectives are generally specific and clear but may involve only lower-level thinking.	Emphasis is on all students learning specific basic skills. Students are taught/assessed at grade level. Easier to identify skills students have and have not mastered.	Objectives are not integrated. Higher-level thinking cannot be assessed as easily. In real life skills overlap; they are not isolated from one another. Problem solving skills are minimized.
Structured assessment tasks which are the same for all students.	Students are given specific guidance in what they are to do. Some students need and respond well to structure. Helps students to learn to conform and follow directions and specifications. Easy to set up assessment criteria. Students are aware of expectations and routines.	Creativity and independence is ignored. Many skills overlap and should not be assessed in isolation. Sets limits on thinking. Usually does not measure skills and knowledge beyond grade level expectations.
Administration is efficient, quick, and easy.	Quickly completed which allows more time for classroom tasks. Less time is needed for teachers to grade. Requires little or no teacher training about how to administer and use.	Efficiency can lead to repetition, boredom, and laziness.

Traditional Assessment

Characteristic	Advantages	Disadvantages
High reliability with low cost.	Reliability is familiar to the public. Fits most school/district budgets. Available and cost effective to use with all students, even in large systems.	While generally reliable, scores can be deceptive in terms of what students really know. Some students are good guessers; others are horrible test takers. Ethnic, economic, regional, or other types of bias may be imbedded in the test.
Scoring is done by computer usually giving a single score on each test or subtest. May be norm-or criterion-referenced.	Easy to score, time efficient, giving a single score. Results are understood by all.	Doesn't show student insight. Doesn't give detailed information about what a student knows. Does not measure creativity. Harder to measure higher-level thinking. Presents narrow view of student ability and achievement.
Desired responses are fixed, usually giving the student one correct choice from a group of options.	Teachers and students know what the right answers are, which are correct, and which are incorrect. Easy to grade.	No opportunity to assess any knowledge that isn't specifically asked. Not open and does not provide for various intelligences and learning styles. Does not allow student to be creative in responses.
Impact on students is varied depending on student attitude, learning style, and stress level.	Pressure may elicit good performance. Concrete sequential students like knowing exact expectations and right or wrong answers. May help students become proficient at test-taking skills. Students may take school more seriously and develop more responsibility for their own learning.	May cause high levels of stress and test anxiety. Not a good means to assess students who are not good test takers. May believe the only things worth learning are the things that are on the test. May cause negative attitudes about assessment. May discourage achievement.

Traditional Assessment

Characteristic	Advantages	Disadvantages
Assessor bias not a problem.	Everyone considers results to be fair. Assessor would not favor or disadvantage anyone while scoring the test.	Assessor cannot judge test bias nor is there any consideration given for different approaches to solving the problem. While assessors are not biased, the test items themselves may be biased giving particular advantage or disadvantage to a given group. The assessor would not have any control over this and no way to remedy the situation.
Does not require teacher planning time for preparation of assessment instrument.	Teachers have too much to do with too little time to accomplish everything. Time can be used for other things rather than developing assessment instruments.	When teachers have no direct involvement in developing the assessment instrument, it is less likely to assess what has actually been taught.
Results easy to explain to parents and the public.	Most adults are familiar with traditional assessments and test scores.	Scores can be misinterpreted. All tests are not scored in the same way and the same numeric score may mean different things on different tests.
Can be designed to go along precisely with state standards and/or district mandates.	Assessment and instruction are aligned. What is being taught is what is being tested.	If the entire curriculum is based only on what is being tested, many important things may not be taught.

Alternative Assessment

Characteristic	Advantages	Disadvantages
Purpose is to show improvement, growth, and what a student knows and can do.	Good for students who don't test well because there are other avenues to show what they know. Gives feedback which points toward the next step in improvement.	May not have required documentation. Not as good for students who don't work well in class but do test well.
Integrated sets of objectives often covering many subject areas, usually focused on higher-order thinking.	More challenging work. Teachers are more likely to focus on higher-level thinking skills because these are being assessed. Gives a way to document higher-level achievement. Can cover many objectives at the same time. Encourages teachers not to teach skills in isolation.	Hard to isolate specific standards. May not know precise skills a student knows and ones he doesn't know. Basic skills may be neglected.
Open-ended tasks that are different for different students.	Addresses different learning styles and intelligences. Encourages creativity and problem solving. More like problems found in "real life." Gives a good picture of what the child actually can do. Student has latitude to demonstrate skills. Meets a wide variety of student interests.	More subjective. Ability to compare one child with the entire group is diminished. Time consuming. Some students are much more comfortable with specific directions and structured tasks to complete. Some students will find it difficult to focus.
Administration and scoring can be time consuming.	The time it takes is worth it if the assessment gives detailed information. May end up assessing fewer students.	Less efficient. Teachers and administrators may be discouraged from using this type of assessment because it is so time consuming. Rubrics must be valid and reliable. Some are not.

Alternative Assessment

Characteristic	Advantages	Disadvantages
Reliability is more difficult to maintain; requires training for scorers.	With sufficient training, scoring can be reliable. Good rubrics make authentic assessments easier to score.	Use of assessment for accountability is diminished. Teacher bias and human error more likely to occur. Training may be costly.
Complex scoring usually involving checklists and rubrics.	Detailed documentation. Able to pinpoint general areas for growth and improvement. Accurately shows strengths and weaknesses that help teachers plan future instruction.	Time consuming to score accurately. Because it is time consuming and requires extensive training, this type of assessment may be too costly for many school districts. Criteria can be difficult to interpret.
Students construct their own response that may be in the form of product, process, or performance.	Better overall assessment of the individual student. Can assess students' best work. Students have ownership in the response.	Responses may be interpreted differently by different scorers.
Not as threatening to the student because assessment tasks are embedded in ongoing instruction.	Less stress for students. Students are more likely to have positive feelings about assessment. Boosts self confidence.	May cause the student to study less and not work as hard. Some students like traditional tests and are not comfortable with other forms of assessment. May lessen competitive drive that motivates some students.

Designing Alternative/Performance Assessment Tasks

> *"I know I should use performance assessments," Ms. Perez confided to a colleague. "It's a big push in our district, but it takes so much time! And I really don't know exactly what they want me to do. My supervisor suggested that the students do individual projects at the end of a unit of study, but isn't that part of their class work? How is that assessment? I'm not sure I understand what this type of assessment actually is or how I am going to implement it in my classroom."*

Ms. Perez's confusion is widespread. There is talk about alternative/performance assessment but many teachers don't know exactly what is meant by this or exactly how they should go about administering those kinds of assessments in their classrooms.

Part of this confusion stems from the terminology itself. When people refer to alternative assessment, they sometimes mean the assessment tasks (such as specific projects, products, or performances) while at other times they may be speaking about the assessment instruments (such as rubrics, checklists, or learning logs). In traditional assessment, we generally have a test and a test score coupled together so there is not as much need to distinguish between the two.

Subsequent chapters in this book give detailed information about the assessment instruments that can be used for alternative assessment. Designing meaningful assessment tasks for students takes careful thought and an organized approach. In doing this, you need to consider the following:

- Your rationale for teaching the unit or information to be assessed
- Standards, benchmarks, objectives, and/or outcomes to be measured by the assessment
- The Enduring Understandings you hope students will have as a result of their learning
- The structure of the assessment task itself
- Criteria that shows students have achieved the desired outcomes

Use the forms on the next three pages to help you design and plan alternative assessment tasks for your students.

At the end of this chapter you will find a Reflection Page about both traditional and alternative assessment. Consider how and when you use these two types of assessment as you complete this form.

Planning an Alternative Assessment Task

Theme or Topic: ______________________________

Overall rationale:

____

____

____

____

Standards, benchmarks, objectives, and/or outcomes:

____

____

____

____

____

____

____

____

____

____

Enduring understandings:

____

____

____

Alternative Assessment Task Outline

Title of task:

Purpose: To assess

Materials: (Include materials needed and how they will be supplied)

Time range allotted for task: (Include time at school and time at home, if applicable)

Student grouping for task: (Individual, pairs, trios, etc.)

Overview/summary of activity:

Detailed description of alternative assessment activity:

Criteria for Assessment Task

Note: These criteria can be the starting point for developing a complex rubric. See Chapter 9.

Project/Product/Performance: ______________________________

Assessment criteria:

1. ______________________________
2. ______________________________
3. ______________________________
4. ______________________________

Project/Product/Performance: ______________________________

Assessment criteria:

1. ______________________________
2. ______________________________
3. ______________________________
4. ______________________________

Scoring or Grading:

____

____

____

____

____

Traditional and Alternative Assessments
Teacher Reflection Page

In my classroom I generally use _____% traditional assessment and _____% alternative assessment.

My reasons for this are:

____

____

____

____

Which characteristics of traditional assessments are characteristics of the assessments I use?

____

____

____

Which characteristics of alternative assessment are characteristics of the assessments I use?

____

____

____

What are my strengths and weaknesses in using alternative assessments?

____

____

____

What are my main reasons for using traditional assessments?

____

____

____

When do I use either type of assessment inappropriately?

____

____

____

Chapter 6
The Assessment/Instruction Cycle

What you teach should be what you assess – before, during, and after instruction!

* *According to the National Excellence Report (1993), elementary gifted students often know between 35% - 50% of the curriculum before they ever begin the school year. Yet many teachers fail to pre-assess such students to see what they already know before instruction begins.*

* *Children who get 50% - 60% on a classroom unit test generally get an F. We rarely look to see what portion of the information they have learned or where their academic holes are. We just put their grades in our grade book and go on to the next unit of study.*

* *If we give a student one zero, it takes 5 scores of 90 or above to bring up his grade to passing level.*

The facts above indicate some of the ways we could use assessment to guide our instruction, but many of us have failed to do so. The way we generally look at assessment assumes some will get it, some will not, and then we'll move on. We rarely use assessment to guide us in what we teach.

In traditional classrooms, teachers complete instruction, then assess, grade, and report. The assessment and reporting are considered events separate from instruction itself. This approach tells students that what we value are grades and test scores. A much better approach is to start planning instruction by looking first at assessment results and then plan our curriculum and instruction based on them.

Teaching and assessing on a continual basis helps students work toward their goals. In a classroom where formative assessments and instruction are interwoven, it is hard to tell where teaching ends and assessing begins. In this type of classroom, students learn that an ability to self-assess, make changes and adjustments based on formative assessment, and improve their own performance is very valuable in growing as a learner. When assessment and instruction are linked in an ongoing cycle, teachers can more easily identify and monitor student progress.

Assessment and instruction can be linked, and this is the goal for many teachers and schools. Student responses, performances, and products can be the logical end of the instructional process and at the same time be the assessment for the teacher to use. Creating your own assessment tasks is usually better than relying on those off-the-shelf because yours will be aligned to your curriculum and standards. This is one of the biggest advantages in using assessments linked directly to instruction.

In this chapter, we explore ways to join assessment and instruction, especially through the use of a curriculum compactor and through a unique final exam. In subsequent chapters, we look further at this topic as we consider portfolios, student self-assessment, learning logs, checklists, rubrics, and RTI progress monitoring forms.

Assessment and Curriculum Compacting

> *I am using curriculum compacting with pre- and post-tests for every math objective. As students show mastery of the standards, they work on more challenging alternate activities. — 5th grade teacher*

One strategy for linking assessment and instruction is curriculum compacting. Developed by Dr. Joseph Renzulli and Linda Smith, this is a process by which students are pre-tested for mastery. Those who already know the material to be studied don't need to do the assigned work. Instead, they are allowed to pursue another activity. Compacting involves identifying the content or skill area and/or the standard or benchmark, pre-assessing, documenting mastery, and providing alternate activities for students who have mastered the material.

This strategy works particularly well in subjects or topics that are easily pre-tested, such as math, spelling, grammar, vocabulary, and map skills. The teacher decides ahead of time what pre-test score or demonstration of the knowledge or skill will be acceptable as mastery.

Directions for Compacting

1. Provide a blank Curriculum Compactor (adapted from the form developed by Linda H. Smith and Dr. Joseph Renzulli) for students. You may want each student to list the items compacted. Another approach is to design a Curriculum Compactor form with the skills, benchmarks, or standards listed for a unit. Students then use the form as a record of their work.

2. Use the Curriculum Compactor form to record all modifications in curriculum.
   - In the left column, record the student's areas of strength, one skill or area of knowledge per box. Standards or benchmarks are good guidelines for the items that go into this column.
   - In the center column, document the student's mastery. This is done through some type of assessment, often (but not always) a pre-test score.
   - In the right column, indicate the activities the student will be engaged in while the rest of the class is working on the skill or benchmark.

3. Alternate activities are usually extensions, enrichment, or acceleration of the same subject area. Sometimes, however, they may be anchor activities from different subject areas or from the student's individual interest area.

4. Each student should be responsible for keeping his or her compactor folder. In it should be all pre-tests and other pertinent data with dates, all compactor forms, and the work from alternate activities.

Helpful Hints

- Unless the student specifically requests it, do not use the time a student "buys" from a strength area to remediate a learning weakness.
- Give students a choice of several alternate learning activities.
- The one choice a student never has is the choice to do nothing!
- Keeping a compactor folder is a good way for students to learn skills in organization and gives practice in taking responsibility.

One of the advantages of curriculum compacting is that it can be structured in many different ways. It is flexible enough to work within the existing framework of a variety of classrooms and teaching styles. Below is one example of a curriculum compactor for an individual student that covers a number of different skills. A blank form is included on the next page. On the next several pages, you will see how a Student Evaluation Form can be used as another type of compactor to assess an entire class and document progress and mastery through pre-tests and post-tests.

CURRICULUM COMPACTOR*

Name ________________________________

Standard or Benchmark Content or Skill Area	Documenting Mastery	Alternate Activities
Properly use verb tenses.	95% on pre-test with fill in the blanks	Write a creative short story underlining verbs that are present tense. or Write a report on local history underlining verbs that are past tense.
Multiply two-digit decimals.	100% on pre-test	Write a series of word problems that require multiplication of decimals. or Make a collage using newspapers or magazines showing the use of decimals in everyday life.
Spell a list of frequently misspelled words.	90% on pre-test of 50 words	Look in a dictionary and find 25 words you do not know how to spell. Along with any words you missed, write these into a humorous poem or story. Underline each and be sure to spell correctly. or Construct a crossword puzzle using these words plus any words you missed on the pre-test.

*Adapted from the form by Linda H. Smith and Dr. Joseph Renzulli

CURRICULUM COMPACTOR

Student's Name ______________________________

Standard or Benchmark Content or Skill Area	Documenting Mastery	Alternate Activities

Reproducible

Using the Student Evaluation Form to Record Student Assessments in Preparation for Curriculum Compacting in One Specific Subject

Math is an ideal subject to differentiate instruction by using curriculum compacting. In math, some specific skills are "black and white" based upon your state's standards, an adopted math series, or your grade level or course scope and sequence. Assessing these skills is a good place to begin compacting.

Once skill areas are listed, a pre-test is given to each student. The pre-test is separated by skill areas with specific questions designed to test knowledge and understanding of the specific skill. Usually 4-5 questions are used to evaluate mastery in each skill area. Students are given ample time to complete the pre-test and are encouraged to just do their best or skip problems that they don't know or that seem confusing. No grade is given for the pre-test. It is simply a way of assessing which students have already mastered specific skill areas and which students need further instruction.

A student's pre-test is marked for accuracy, and a Student Evaluation Form is filled out. From the form, a student can readily see if he or she has mastered a skill area. "Yes" is checked if a specific skill area has been mastered prior to instruction and "No" is checked if a specific skill area has not been mastered prior to instruction. Depending upon the skills and a student's past math knowledge, he or she may have mastered one or many of the skills in a particular unit.

When a particular skill is taught on a particular day, students check their Student Evaluation Forms. Students who have shown mastery have "compacted out" of listening to the instruction for that day. These students are free to choose enrichment/ extension/acceleration anchor activities planned for them while instruction on the day's skill takes place in the classroom with those students who need the help. Therefore, a teacher may be instructing a small group of students or may have a majority of the class based upon the pre-test results. This naturally uses the flexible grouping strategy based upon instructional needs of the class.

Instruction continues in this manner until the unit is completed and a final chapter test is given. The chapter test is formatted in the same way as the pre-test. Again, the Student Evaluation Form is marked. The obvious goal is to have all skill areas marked "Yes" at the end of the unit of study. Students can easily see the improvement that has taken place and can celebrate the knowledge obtained. Students who still have skill areas marked "No" can receive more intense interventions in these targeted areas.

The key to compacting is to remember that the teacher sets the mastery level for the standards. If a particular lesson requires that everyone listen to the whole group instruction, so be it. If a particular lesson allows every student to choose an alternate activity, so be it. Examples of a Student Evaluation Form, a test that could be used as a pre- or post-test, Alternative Activities Instructions for students, and an Alternate Activities Checklist for students are on the following pages.

Student Evaluation Form

Name ____

Date of pre-test ____________ Date of post-test __________

Standard or Objective	Test Items	Pre-test		Post-test	
		No	Yes	No	Yes
3.1 Exploring multiplication patterns and properties	1, 2, 3, 4				
3.2 Using rounding to estimate products	5, 6, 7, 8				
3.3 Multiply by one-digit and two-digit numbers	9, 10, 11, 12				
3.4 Use the distributive property to multiply	13, 14, 15, 16				
3.5 Decide whether to use paper, pencil, calculator, or mental math when multiplying	17				
3.6 Explore patterns with multiples	18, 19, 20, 21				
3.7 Solve multiple-step problems	22				
3.8 Solve problems by guessing and checking	23				

Math Pre-test or Post-test: Multiplying Whole Numbers

Name ______________________________

3.1 Exploring multiplication patterns and properties
Find each product. Use mental math.

1. 30 x 60 ________
2. 20 x 20 ________
3. 3 x 80 ________
4. 100 x (4 x 3) ________

3.2 Using rounding to estimate products
Estimate each product.

5. 52 x 17 ________
6. 91 x 15 ________
7. 5 x 76 ________
8. 686 x 36 ________

3.3 Multiply by one-digit and two-digit numbers
Find each product.

9. 205 x 4
10. 52 x 38
11. 137 x 16
12. 72 x 55

3.4 Use the distributive property to multiply
Find each product. Use the distributive property.

13. 18 x 99 ________
14. 103 x 15 ________
15. 102 x 11 ________
16. 497 x 5 ________

3.5 Decide whether to use paper/pencil, calculator, or mental math

17. Which method of calculation is the best for finding the product of 439 and 568 quickly? Underline your answer.

a. mental math b. guessing and checking c. calculator d. paper/pencil

3.6 Explore patterns with multiples.

Find the LCM for each set of numbers

18. 3 and 4 ____________
19. 6 and 10 ____________
20. 2 and 7 ____________
21. 4, 5 and 8 ____________

3.7 Solve multiple-step problems.

Solve each problem. Use the 5-step plan and strategy to help you.

22. Adam went to the art museum. He spent $3.75 for admission to the museum, twice that much on gifts at the gift shop, and the rest on lunch. Adam spent $15.04 all together. How much did Adam spend at the gift shop? How much did he spend on lunch?

______________ at the gift shop ______________ on lunch

3.8 Solve problems by checking and guessing.

Solve each problem. Use the 5-step plan and the guess-and-check strategy to help you.

23. Jenny rode her bike 63 miles in all. She rode twice as many miles on paved road as she did on dirt road. How many miles did she ride on paved road?

___________ miles on paved road

Alternate Activities Instructions: Catalog Project

Please read carefully!!

1. You must show me the selection you will be working on each day on your Alternate Activities Checklist before you begin working on your selected activity. If you do not have the checklist with you, you will do the regular class work for the day.

2. You will be allowed to work on your Alternate Activity (give location where student will be working). I will monitor your progress from time to time. I will try to check with you for 5 or 10 minutes each day to answer questions and guide you in your work.

3. It is extremely important that you are on your best behavior when you are working on your Alternate Activity. Your voice should be no louder than a whisper if you need to talk to someone.

4. I have basic supplies such as scissors, tape, markers, construction paper, newspapers, catalogs, and glue sticks available for you. You may need to bring other materials if any are required for your individual project.

5. Take pride in the work you do for your Alternate Activity. This should be quality work and should reflect higher-level thinking and extension of your knowledge.

6. Some projects require research outside the classroom. If you need to go to the media center or to another part of the school, make sure you sign out so I will know where you are. Only one student may be gone at a time.

7. You must monitor your own time as you do your Alternate Activity. You may need to allow approximately 5-10 minutes at the end of class to clean up and organize your materials for the next day's work.

8. The one choice you never have is the choice to do nothing! Learning time is too valuable.

I have read the instructions and am aware of what is expected of me when I compact the curriculum and work on Alternate Activities.

Student signature ____

Parent signature ____

Alternate Activities Checklist: Catalogs

Put in the blank the date that you begin an activity. Circle the activity number when you complete it.

_________ 1. Look through a collection of catalogs to find out how many ways math skills and processes are used and presented. Make a list of all you can find (minimum 10, maximum 100). Categorize your list, and present your findings in a graphic organizer such as a chart, Venn diagram, etc.

_________ 2. Select three pages in one catalog that contain similar items. Determine the average cost per page. Repeat with several other catalogs. Then show your findings on a graph.

_________ 3. Develop plans for a new type of catalog. This can be as creative as you want and can include technology. Write your proposal for this new type of catalog, and develop a few sample pages. Your proposal should be persuasive, organized, logical, and at least a page in length.

_________ 4. Prepare a checklist or rubric that class members can use when they evaluate catalogs and/or select products from catalogs. Your checklist must contain at least 10 well-stated criteria.

_________ 5. Use advertisements from local newspapers to compare and contrast prices in stores with prices in catalogs. Be sure to include the cost of shipping and handling and the cost of transportation for local shopping. Compare the costs of at least 10 different products that can be purchased in both stores and catalogs. Be sure to show how you arrived at your conclusions.

_________ 6. Create your own catalog (8-10 pages) featuring products of interest to people in your age group or to your family. Write catalog descriptions, draw illustrations, list prices, construct an order form, and include shipping and handling for all items. Take sample orders from 5 different people using copies of your order form. Which items were the most popular? Which items were not ordered at all? What would you do differently in your next catalog?

_________ 7. Activity of your own choosing: describe below. This must be approved by your teacher before you begin.

Measuring Intangibles

A report on the business news segment of National Public Radio discussed the increasing recognition from businesses that intangibles significantly influence the bottom line. Such intangibles include long term goals, research and development, quality, worker satisfaction, effort and motivation, teamwork, customer services, and excellence. Further, businesses are realizing that their value is more than what can be shown by the old measurements of input and output. The financial meltdown of 2007-2009 was caused by many intangible factors as well as bank balance sheets. The question is how to measure the intangibles.

It seems that education faces much the same question. Sometimes the approach to educational assessment seems like the corporate focus on the bottom line and short term profits without looking to other things. That one significant teacher who cared, the importance of persistence, effort, and character are just as important as test scores but are much harder to quantify. We need to remember that these things have value that sometimes cannot be measured.

One high school English teacher valued some intangibles when she crafted an unusual final exam for her 10th and 11th graders. While assessment cannot always be this unique, this is an excellent example of incorporating the intangibles we value into the assessments we give our students. Below you will see this teacher's comments about why she did this activity. On the following page you will see a copy of the "Final Exam" her students received. Finally, you will read her reflections and helpful hints.

An Alternative Final Exam

This idea was inspired by a "Dear Abby" letter. In the letter the writer commented on the death of her grandmother. While going through the woman's personal things, the family found an autobiography written by her as a final project in high school. The letter writer expressed her appreciation for the teacher who had assigned it, as it gave the family a view of their grandmother as a young person. It was a gift and a delight to see her in this new way.

Intrigued, I discussed the letter with my 10th and 11th graders and had them consider what their grandchildren would gain from reading about them as teenagers. It was a great brainstorming session! At the end of the period, I told them that instead of a final exam they would be writing their own autobiographies for their grandchildren. They loved the idea of not having a final but were hesitant about writing an autobiography. They were given the following instructions:

Autobiography Final Exam

This project consists of two parts:

a) Written, due the day before finals (assigned two months in advance)
b) Oral, to be presented on the day of exams

Written requirements:

1. No less than 10 and no more than 20 pages
2. Must be typed in a standard 10 or 12 point font
3. Must be written in first person
4. No invented events. This only hurts your grandchildren or yourself.
5. If an event is too personal to share, make two versions of your autobiography. The edited one can go to me. Save the real one for yourself.
6. Give real names and dates. Those are things you forget as you get older and wish you'd recorded.
7. Use good descriptive adjectives that will give a vivid picture of you and your life.
8. Follow good writing form learned in class this year.
9. Proofread your rough draft before making a final copy.
10. Divide your autobiography into chapters, giving each an interesting and/or creative name.
11. Have a title page with a title that summarizes your philosophy of life and would make us want to read it if we ran across it cleaning out your files.
12. Late papers will not be accepted without approval from the Assistant Principal. (As with any final exam, you must have a doctor's excuse.)

Oral presentation requirements:

1. The presentation must be between 5-10 minutes in length.
2. You may share a life-changing incident from your autobiography or comment on the process of writing the autobiography. Include what you learned about yourself and/or your family while doing this.
3. You may refer to your notes but not read the autobiography to us word for word.

Student name:

Due date - Written autobiography: ________________

Due date - Oral presentation: ________________

Parent signature: ____

Reflections and Helpful Hints

The autobiographies were excellent. The lowest grades on papers turned in on time were two C's. Those students did the assignment but didn't follow directions or proofread. Two students tried to turn in their papers late. The Assistant Principal met with both of them. Neither could verify a doctor's appointment or justify the lateness of their paper, so both received a "0" on that portion of the exam.

Criteria for assessment included:

- Followed directions regarding number of pages, chapters, etc.
- Vivid and clear use of language
- Writing style
- Proofreading
- Showed span of life from birth to present
- Self-reflection in telling about events and philosophy

Student evaluations of this assignment were enthusiastic. Most agreed that they found it daunting, but if they worked on it steadily it wasn't that hard. They learned a great deal about themselves and had some bonding moments with their families as they did research about their own lives. Some of the papers were astonishingly candid. Many students made great effort and were motivated to find out more about who they actually were.

Most kids went overtime in the oral section of the exam. They were eager to share about themselves and what they had researched, learned, and accomplished. There was about a 50/50 split as to whether they chose to talk about a life-changing incident or the process of writing the autobiography.

"Nuts and Bolts" issues:

1. It is important to clear this type of exam with the administration before you assign it, because it doesn't fit the standard idea of a final exam.

2. Give the students enough time to do the assignment. Mention it during the weeks they are to be working on it.

3. Reserve evenings at home to read these papers. It does take time, but it is much more interesting than reading and grading a traditional final exam.

4. Be specific about assessment criteria and share the criteria with the students beforehand. Decide how much the written product will count and how much the oral presentation will count.

5. Require student and parent signatures on the assignment when they first start. This assures that parents will know about the "exam" and will encourage students not to procrastinate.

6. Make sure you are available for questions or discussions with students as they work on the assignment.

Assessment
Teacher Reflection Page

1. What skills, benchmarks, or standards in your current curriculum lend themselves to curriculum compacting? List below along with ways you could assess mastery.

Skills, Benchmarks, or Standards	How to Assess Mastery

2. Brainstorm ways you might be able to include intangibles in your assessment activities. List your ideas below.

Reproducible

Chapter 7
Reporting and Documenting Student Progress

Got your report card? What did she give you?

Grades and Report Cards

> *I have a student who has a depth of understanding about the literature we are studying considerably beyond any other student I teach. She reads far more than assigned, yet she doesn't turn in written work and is incredibly unorganized with her time. This makes me wonder if grades should be based on knowledge or output, on effort or understanding? It is a dilemma.*
>
> *—AP English teacher*

How important and accurate are grades? Sometimes they are not as accurate or as important as we might think. Artist Mia Lynn, the designer of the famous Vietnam War Memorial in Washington, D.C., tells an interesting story about a grade she received in school. Her design for the Memorial was done when she was only 20 years old and was originally produced for a class project in college. As unbelievable as it may sound, her professor gave her design a **B**. Regardless of the grade it had gotten, she decided to submit it to the contest for the design of the Memorial. 1,400 other designs were also submitted. As we all know, her design won, and this Memorial has become one of the most famous and most visited in Washington. It makes one wonder how accurate that **B** actually was!

Grading is one of the strangest things we do in education. It is difficult to know how a particular grade is arrived at because the process of grading daily work and then giving a report card grade has little if any uniformity, even within the same school. There is little agreement among educators as to what should be included or counted in a grade, whether grades are criterion- or norm-referenced, or whether grades should be used as motivators and rewards or should simply report student progress. The two scenarios above highlight these issues.

Nevertheless, it appears we will have grades and report cards for the foreseeable future. How, then, do we properly assess and accurately communicate while using them? The primary purpose of grading should be to provide accurate and understandable feedback that students can use to improve their performance. Additionally, parents need grades to learn how their children are doing in school. Grades should serve as a consistent form of communication between home and school.

Traditionally, teaching has focused heavily on grades, and there is pressure on students to earn good grades. At the same time, grade inflation is rampant in American schools, and grades do not always reflect top achievement or who is working to his or her potential. Many gifted and high-achieving students are terrified of getting anything other than an A, but often these same students get A's while putting forth little or no effort. If such students go all the way through elementary and middle school getting A's but never putting forth much effort or working very hard, they are actually *under*achievers!

Parents may find it hard to understand various forms of alternative assessment, especially when there is narrative feedback but no letter or number grade. They want their kids to be graded in the same way THEY were. Teachers need to explain how expectations for students have changed. Giving a grade at the end of a unit of study or at the end of the grading period is not nearly as helpful as guidance during a project, giving students ongoing opportunities to refine their products during the process, and culminating reflections on what has been learned. There needs to be a definitive connection between project assessment criteria and the grades students receive.

Some defend the extensive use of grades claiming that students are not motivated to work without them. Yet a number of teachers believe that giving grades is not an effective way to motivate and evaluate students. In fact, because teachers grade in so many different ways, students with more than one teacher get confused about how grades are figured in the first place. In fact, the process of assigning grades is inherently subjective. Thus, the age-old question of "What grade did you give me?" rather than "What grade did I earn?"

Alternative Suggestions for Grades

1. Come to an agreement as an entire school about what is indicated or assessed by a report card grade. For instance, your school may decide that individual achievement will be the only thing the grade shows. Effort, participation, attitude, working with others, etc. would then be shown separately. Conversely, all of the items listed above could be included in the grade on the report card. The important thing is for everyone to be in agreement about what is included and what is not.

2. Grades should reflect a sample of student work. We don't have to grade every piece of paper and put the score in the grade book! Teachers are often exhausted and overwhelmed because of all the grading they think they must do. Grade some work, but have your students self-assess other work. Check to make sure the work is done without always putting a grade or number of points on it. We have trained students and parents to expect grades for everything — we can also "un-train" them.

3. Enter classwork grades in pencil or do not enter them immediately into your computerized grade book. This gives the message that they are temporary. You can change an initial grade if you see improvement in a skill over the duration of the grading period. Recent marks usually reflect student progress in a skill or concept. Entering classwork grades in pencil is also a good strategy to use with curriculum compacting. When a student "tests out" of classwork, a grade in pencil indicates that work will be done in an alternate (more challenging) activity.

4. Offer students opportunities to improve their marks. If a student re-does a paper or assignment, some credit should be given for the learning that has taken place. Most students will learn from the mistakes they made the first time and will do better on the second attempt. Isn't this type of learning what we hope will happen?

5. Weight grades by topics or skills. The most important skill should receive the most weight. Often we grade each assignment as if all were of equal importance. This is rarely the case.

6. Watch for the effect one very low grade (or a zero) has on the overall grade. Sometimes one low score can make the entire grade lower than it should be to reflect the student's true performance. You may want to try a median score rather than an average.

7. Grade according to established criteria rather than establishing preordained quotas for grades. All students should have the possibility of getting **A**'s if they all have earned them according to standards-based criteria. If all students reach the highest standard, all should get the highest grade.

8. Explain how your students' work is going to be assessed before they begin an assignment or task. The criteria for grading should never be a mystery.

9. Use some alternative assessment and reporting strategies in place of, or in addition to, grades and report cards. Several alternative methods are described throughout this chapter.

10. Make sure grades are indicative of students' skills and progress in different types of activities. Test grades should be balanced by classwork, homework, projects, and performances.

11. Decide how or whether formative assessments will be reflected in report card grades.

12. Include a number and a letter grade with the number indicating the level. For example, 1 might indicate below grade level, 2 could indicate on grade level, while 3 or 4 might indicate advanced or very advanced work. Report card grades would then look like B4 or A2. This reporting strategy works particularly well with tiered lessons and units.

Standards-Based Report Cards

All states have grade-level standards, and teaching these standards is the goal for every teacher. Because of the importance of the standards, it makes sense that grades reflect the progress each student makes toward mastering them. Standards-based report cards do exactly that. They show how far along each child is in mastering specific knowledge and skills that all are expected to learn.

A standards-based report card lists the most important skills students should learn in each subject at a particular grade level. Instead of letter grades, students receive a separate mark for each standard that shows how well they have mastered the skills. The marks might show whether the student is advanced, proficient, basic, or below basic for each standard, or they might be numbers representing whether students meet, exceed, or approach each standard.

Standards-based grading ensures that teachers cover certain topics and that students learn necessary material at each grade level. Grading gives indicators of student achievement on the standards and measures each student against a stated set of criteria. This eliminates one student being compared to other students. It also does away with the practice of averaging scores received during a grading period.

Standards-based report cards can be confusing or overwhelming to students and parents. Educators must make sure the list of standards on the report card is not too long and that each standard is understandable. Another area of controversy is that many students do not get to the proficient or advanced level until the end of the school year. This is difficult to understand, especially for students and parents who are accustomed to straight **A**'s!

Grades and Report Cards
Teacher Reflection Page

Discuss with another teacher or with your grade level or department:

- What components do you currently include in your grades?

- In what ways are our grading systems similar? How are they different? Should we try to make them more consistent with one another?

- Do these items reflect what is really important in students' work and progress?

- Could we improve our grading system and/or report cards so that they communicate student learning more clearly? In what ways?

- Have you used standards-based report cards? What are the pros and cons of using them?

Monitoring Student Progress using the Response to Intervention (RTI) Approach

RTI began as a special education initiative that emphasizes the need for intervention strategies in the general education classroom. It was introduced in the 2004 reauthorization of the Individuals with Disabilities Education Act (IDEA).

It recommends intervention services and the use of best practices and strategies in the regular classroom before a referral for special education services. However, it provides a framework for responding to the needs of all students in the regular classroom. Thus it is for all teachers, not just special education teachers or a small RTI team.

The RTI approach structures research-based interventions for a variety of students, including those with academic delays or behavioral problems, gifted students, and English Language Learners and monitors their progress frequently to see if the interventions are helping each student succeed in school.

The approach should include both pre-assessment to establish a baseline and formative assessments for monitoring student progress.

In the RTI approach, schools are likely to have:

- Academic and behavioral screening for all students
- Targeted research-based interventions aimed at addressing individual student's problem areas and needs that were identified during the screening process
- Frequent monitoring of student progress in order to assess how well a specific intervention is working.

The RTI approach points the way to individualized, differentiated instruction for all students along with continuous formative assessment so that we can readily see which strategies work with an individual student and which do not.

Pre-assessment

- An essential element of differentiation and RTI
- Necessary in order to meet the diverse needs of each student
- Specifies each student's starting point before instruction begins
- Shows learning differences among students (important for differentiation)
- Indicates when there is a need for targeted research-based interventions (important for RTI)

Formative Assessment

- Assessment while instruction and/or student work is going on
- Shows student progress toward a learning goal (RTI progress monitoring)
- Alerts teachers to students' misunderstandings and gives evidence of their need to learn something again or in a different way (differentiation)

For more information on monitoring student progress and the RTI approach, see *Differentiation, RTI and Achievement: How They Work Together.* Carolyn Coil. Pieces of Learning. 2009.

Student-Led Parent Conferences

One of the main purposes of grades and report cards is to share student progress with parents. A report card may do this to a minimal degree, but more often it becomes a cause for punishment, a means to a tangible reward, or it is used to give parents "bragging rights" with their friends and family.

A student-led conference is a better way to truly share with parents what their child is learning and how he or she is progressing. In a student-led conference, students describe their progress to their parents. They usually pick representative work samples and, while showing these, describe their specific accomplishments, tell what they have learned, and identify mistakes or failures.

In a student-led conference, the parents, the teacher, and the student jointly:

- Review the student's work
- Compare this work to expected standards and benchmarks
- Discuss strengths and areas of growth
- Target specific weaknesses and areas needing improvement
- Produce goals and identify new benchmarks
- Develop a learning plan for the future

In this type of conference, the student serves as the chair. Guidelines for a student-led conference are on the next page. Page 85 is a Post Conference Summary page.

Guidelines/Agenda for a Student-Led Conference

1. The student welcomes everyone.

2. The teacher and the student review the conference process and may present a written agenda.

3. The student shares selected work samples. These are chosen beforehand by the student, often with input from the teacher.

4. Student, parents, and teacher all share the strengths they see in the student's work. Strengths may be listed on paper as they are discussed.

5. Student, teacher, and parent each share one or two areas on which the student needs to work. These areas are listed and, if there are several mentioned, they may be rank ordered.

6. Both strengths and weaknesses are discussed by all in attendance. Students are usually very good judges of the quality of their own work and what they need to do to improve it.

7. The student comes up with two or three learning goals for the future. Often these are based on state standards and guidelines. Each person explains how she or he will help support working toward these goals. It is important that everyone involved in the conference understand what the student's future learning goals and outcomes are. When this happens, instead of bringing home a packet or notebook filled with papers for their parents to go through without really knowing what they are looking at, students will bring home evidence of how well they are doing in working toward their learning goals.

8. A timetable or schedule is set for working on these goals.

9. The teacher answers questions and summarizes the future directions for the student's learning that have been discussed and agreed upon. The teacher may need to give guidance and answer questions, but all participants in the conference need to listen to what all others are saying.

10. The student ends the conference and thanks everyone for coming and for their participation.

For a student-led conference to go well, it is extremely helpful for parents to have some background information about what goes on in the classroom and the grade level expectations and standards. In general, when parents see the value of hearing about school progress from students themselves, they buy into the whole process.

The reproducible form on the next page may be used as a Summary Form at the end of a Student-Led Conference.

Post Conference Summary Page

Student name ______________________________ Date ____________

Work samples shared: ______________________________

____

____

____

Student's strengths: ______________________________

____

____

____

Skills, attitudes, or knowledge that need improvement: ______________

____

____

____

Learning goals: ______________________________

____

____

____

Plan of action (with dates): ______________________________

____

____

____

Signatures of those attending conference: ______________________________

____

____

Student Journals and Learning Logs

Another way to record and to report student progress is by having the students keep journals and learning logs. One type of weekly journal requires students to write learning goals for the week on one page, with their reflections and evaluation of their work on the facing page. This type of learning log is an excellent follow-up to a student-led conference.

Learning Goals for week of October 10-15	Reflections and evaluation of my work
1. Identify a variety of geometric figures	I found most of the figures in the math book.
2. Show how they are used in the real world.	I did an online search and found other types of figures.
3. Find examples of figures in nature or man-made objects.	I had trouble finding any information about where these are in the real world. Nothing really said that. But I looked around and could see some figures just in the classroom and in my yard.
4. Construct sample figures.	A couple of my models fell apart.
5. Write an informational report on what I have learned.	I haven't finished my written report. I guess I'll turn it in late.
	I would give myself a B for finding and making the figures and doing research on them but an F so far on my report since I haven't turned it in.

There are many format variations for student learning logs. It is important to help the student record what he or she has learned, what the goals and objectives were in doing the work, and the method of showing where the student is heading in the future. In any type of learning log, the process of thinking and analyzing is much more important than the form upon which it is recorded. It is the "Reflections" column that causes difficulty for students. Work with your students to practice thinking and writing about their reflections about learning. This concept will be new to most of them. Following are learning log forms:

- Two different blank forms for learning logs similar to the one above.
- A sample long-range project learning log and a blank form for the same.

A Student Log for ______________________________ Activity

Name ______________________________

Date: __________________

Activity description ____

____

____

What I learned ____

____

____

Ways to improve next time ____

____

____

My overall rating for the activity _______

Teacher comments and evaluation____

____

____

____

____

Grade _______

My Learning Log

Name ______________________________ Subject ______________________

Learning Goals for Week of

____

Reflections and evaluation of my work

Some of my goals for next week are:

Reproducible

Record of Work for Product or Performance

Date	Work Planned	Work Actually Done	Adjustments to Plan for next day	Reflections on my work (Difficulties, strengths, surprises)
Monday	Find books and other information on the topic at home and at the library.	Found one book at home. My mom couldn't take me to the library.	Now I need to go to the library tomorrow.	My mom was too busy and she is making me get behind. I wish I could drive.
Tuesday	Take notes from all sources. See what's on the Internet that I could use.	Went to the library and found a book and 2 news articles. Surfed the Internet but didn't see anything useful.	I need to work on the notes tomorrow.	I saw a lot of cool stuff on the Net but nothing that will help me with this report and project.
Wednesday	Begin writing rough draft. Plan visuals to go with written report.	Took notes from the books. Started making a collage.	I want to do the whole rough draft tomorrow.	My collage is good. It is turning out better than I thought. But I wish the rough draft was finished.
Thursday	Finish rough draft. Ask someone to proofread. Work on visuals.	Finished the collage.	Now I have to do the rough draft and the final report this weekend.	I hate homework on weekends. I leave the stuff I don't like to do until the last minute.
Weekend	Do final report. Finish visuals. Put together in folder.	Rough draft done. My dad proofread it. I got my folder and decorated it.	I have to do the whole final written report on Monday night.	I wish this assignment was done. My collage is the best!
Monday	Check to make sure everything is ready to be turned in tomorrow.	Written report finished. Everything is in a folder.	I am ready to turn this in.	I'm glad the teacher made us plan a "cushion day" in our projected work plan. That is the only reason this will be turned in on time.

From Encouraging Achievement by Carolyn Coil, Pieces of Learning

Reproducible

Record of Work for Product or Performance

Date	Work Planned	Work Actually Done	Adjustments to Plan for Next Day	Reflections on my work (Difficulties, Strengths, Surprises)

Reproducible

Classroom Observations

With so much emphasis on standardized tests, it is important to remember that one of the best sources of information about what each child can do is the classroom teacher. Teachers continually work with students, collect student products, see students working in groups, and have one-on-one relationships with them.

To use a media analogy, teacher observations can provide a full-length film while at best a test only provides a snapshot. Consider how much more information and insight you can usually gain from viewing a movie as compared to seeing one photo.

The biggest problem with classroom observations is that they seem to be so subjective. In order to deal with this problem, teachers need tools to transfer their ongoing classroom observations into valid assessment instruments.

A good classroom observation assessment instrument:

- Lists learning objectives
- Establishes clear observable criteria for accomplishing the objectives
- Makes a rating scale from which to judge the criteria

There are many ways to record your observations. A simple index card or half-page form works well for day-to-day classroom observations. These can be kept in a file box alphabetically by student name. Blank forms for your use are on page 92.

Classroom Observation Record

Student's name: ______________________________

Activity: Small group discussion

Learning objectives:

1. To understand the impact of inventions on daily life
2. To convey one's ideas through class discussion

Criteria: Rating (1-3)

1. Discusses at least two different inventions ______
2. Gives an example of how each impacts daily life ______
3. Articulates ideas so they are easily understood ______

Comments:

Classroom Observation Record

Student's name: ______________________________

Activity: ____________________________________

Learning objectives:

1. ____
2. ____

Criteria: Rating (1-3)

1. ______________________________ ______
2. ______________________________ ______
3. ______________________________ ______

Comments:

Classroom Observation Record

Student's name: ______________________________

Activity: ____________________________________

Learning objectives:

1. ____
2. ____

Criteria: Rating (1-3)

1. ______________________________ ______
2. ______________________________ ______
3. ______________________________ ______

Comments:

Reproducible.

Portfolios

> *"I've just received portfolios from my students' third grade teacher," exclaimed Ms. Barnes as she looked through her materials. She was beginning to get her room set up for her 4th graders who were arriving next week. "I've never had portfolios to look through before I even meet the kids. I think this will be really helpful in getting to know them and in seeing where I should start my instruction this year."*
>
> *"Just one more thing to do!" sighed Mr. Mendoza. "I don't know how I'll ever get a portfolio put together for every kid I teach. I didn't do well with this last year! I wish we'd just have the end-of-course test and not worry about anything else."*

The two teachers quoted above view portfolios with quite different attitudes. One sees them as helpful and useful as she begins planning for her students. The other sees them as more work. These varied viewpoints are typical depending on one's experience and background.

Good portfolios do not just happen. They take much effort on the part of teachers and students. They require conferencing with students and other teachers and time to help students formulate both the process and procedures for developing their portfolios. Additionally, a system of assessment through portfolios needs administrative support and parent understanding in order to be successful.

Portfolios are highly flexible instructional and assessment tools. In general, they are collections of student work representing a selection of performances and/or products. The concept of having a portfolio is derived from the visual and performing arts tradition of showcasing artists' accomplishments and selected works and is easily adapted to a school situation showcasing student work.

Why Portfolios?

There are a number of benefits for using portfolios:

- To assemble student work that reflects the standards and objectives of the school, grade level, or school district
- To help students become aware of their progress and improvement in learning over the course of a grading period or school year
- To encourage students to plan for and assess their own learning
- To give teachers insight and information about student growth over a period of time
- To show the student's role in constructing his or her own understanding of concepts, knowledge, and skills

- To support team teaching and cooperative learning in which students and teachers all comment on work in progress or work completed
- To give teachers an idea of each student's progress and abilities from year to year
- To help students become independent and autonomous learners by having them select, correct, and reflect on the work that goes into a portfolio
- To foster parent involvement and understanding of the learning process beyond looking at a single grade on a report card

Sample Types of Portfolios

- Process Folio
  Students keep the first draft along with corrections that were made and include it along with subsequent drafts in process folios. This helps both teacher and student see progress in learning. This approach is especially useful in a writing portfolio.
- Kindergarten Portfolio
  This portfolio shows each child's growth in the areas of art, writing, language arts, and math from the beginning, middle, and end of the school year. It might include a self portrait, a sample of writing numbers 1-25 or 1-100, letters and sounds a child knows, and creative writing samples to show the child's transition from creative to traditional spelling.
- Student-Growth Portfolios (Progress Monitoring)
  This portfolio takes work at specific times to show progress through the year. Collect work samples at the beginning of the year to determine a baseline. Require students to reflect upon their growth periodically. Students track their progress along a growth continuum. This results in internal motivation because students can see they are in control of their own academic success.
- Learning Records/Running Records
  This type of portfolio contains cumulative accounts of progress and beginning points for new endeavors. Students can see where they have been and where they are headed. A standardized format collects evidence of student progress throughout the year. Formative assessments lead to summative assessments by the end of the school year. Parents and students can write descriptions of the progress they have seen through the portfolios.
- Digital Portfolios
  These portfolios can include video presentations, podcasts, contributions to a website, blogs, digital pictures, written documents, PowerPoint presentations, etc. It shows evidence of a student's learning in one subject or more. Films or videos students have produced, videos of student performances, digital animation, evidence of cooperative projects done with others on the Internet, and projects done for audiences beyond the school or classroom can be included.

Portfolios and Assessment

Research shows students see most assessment as something done to them by someone else. They have little knowledge of what is actually involved in evaluating their work. Portfolios provide a structure for involving students in developing criteria for evaluation and taking ownership of that criteria.

The contents of a portfolio along with teacher observations and teacher records will show progress toward the standards and/or individual learning goals. Portfolios may contain work in progress and a student's evaluation of his or her strengths and weaknesses. They can be used to demonstrate a student's work at the beginning of the learning process and at the end to show how far this student has progressed. One advantage of using portfolios is that they will most likely document improvement over time even if the student only picks his best work because, in general, a student's best work keeps getting better.

Portfolios can be passed on from teacher to teacher and from grade level to grade level. Teachers have to coordinate and collaborate with one another for it to be an effective practice.

A Portfolio Rubric or Table of Contents

Portfolios are a good vehicle to use for student self-assessment. It is helpful to have a portfolio Table of Contents and rubric or checklist that allows the student to evaluate the portfolio. The same rubric may be used by the teacher.

The Table of Contents for the portfolio acts as an inventory, guideline, and student self-reflection tool. It can be revised when choices are made concerning what goes in the portfolio. A statement of goals for a certain period of time can be included and revised after the goals are met or the time period is reached. Each piece of writing may have a response written by a peer. There can be a student's self-reflection about anything in the portfolio. There can be a self-evaluation showing what the student feels the portfolio reveals about him or her.

A reproducible form to use as a Portfolio Table of Contents is on page 95.

Portfolio Table of Contents

Standards/
Learning Goals: ______________________________

____

____

Date Description of Item What I Learned

Item 1 ______________________________

Item 2 ______________________________

Item 3 ______________________________

Item 4 ______________________________

Item 5 ______________________________

Item 6 ______________________________

Item 7 ______________________________

Item 8 ______________________________

Item 9 ______________________________

Item 10 ______________________________

Conclusions: ______________________________

____

____

Student's Name: ______________________________

Questions Before You Begin

Many teachers begin using portfolios with their students without thinking through the process ahead of time. It is helpful to consider the following questions before you begin.

- What will it look like?
- How will it be structured?
- What should go in it?
- What will best show progress toward learning goals?
- Will it show only the best work (showcase portfolio) or will it show work that documents improvement?
- How and when will work samples be selected for the portfolio?
- What standards will be used to evaluate the portfolio?
- How much will the portfolio be counted in the final assessment, grade, or evaluation of the work done in the class?
- How will the assessment criteria reflect excellence, effort, and growth?

Chapter 8
About Rubrics: What are They Anyway?

I hear they make you see red!

Known for encouraging student products, I was approached about developing a workshop on designing and using rubrics. Not exactly sure I wanted to do this on my own, I invited a colleague to present along with me. Trudi's 5th grade team had been setting goals and writing criteria all year to meet our state standards. Together, I figured, we'd be fine.

Not so! After spending an hour trying to map out the workshop, we threw up our hands in despair! Calling the person who had originally approached me, I wailed, "We can't do this! We can't even agree on what a rubric IS!

— K-8 Gifted Education Teacher

Just what **is** a rubric? Simply, it's a scoring guide and a way of organizing criteria that describes expectations of student work and measures performance proficiency.

The term "rubric" comes from the Latin word "ruber" for *red.* At one time, red earth or "rubrica terra" was used to mark a thing of importance. After monks in the 15th century used large red letters to begin each major section of an illuminated manuscript, the term "rubric" came to mean the headings for major sections of a book. Today, a rubric assigns an articulated rating scale to those expectations or criteria designated as important in student work.

Teacher Assessment Using Rubrics

Teachers have always known what a good piece of work should look like but usually in a very generalized way. A good rubric helps teachers grade all types of products and performances more fairly since rubrics require teachers to be much more precise about their expectations. Designing specific performance criteria allows teachers to define clearly what achievement targets they want students to hit. It is a more systematized way of doing something teachers in the past have done only intuitively. As their expectations and standards become more consistent and uniform, the grades they give become much more defensible. Students and teachers alike are much more clear about how student work will be evaluated.

When teachers use specific criteria to grade student products and performances and give feedback based on this criteria, students have much more useful feedback than they receive with a mere letter or number grade. Rubrics give students an understanding of the meaning behind the grade.

As more and more teachers use performance assessments and develop rubrics, they are sharing what they have developed with each other. Many school districts now have sets of common scoring rubrics that may be used throughout a grade level or department, throughout a school, or throughout a school district. As a result, the use of rubrics has helped educators create standardized assessment criteria upon which many teachers can agree and can share.

Self-Assessment and Peer Assessment Using Rubrics

With rubrics to guide them, students are more likely to produce higher quality work. They understand what excellent work looks like. They know what the criteria are for this level of work. When used as formative assessments, rubrics help students see concrete ways to improve their work in order to meet the higher standards.

Ultimately, students will examine the criteria in a rubric as they work on a product or performance, and the criteria should point the way toward producing a quality piece of work.

Thus students can use rubrics to evaluate their own work, either to check on quality before it is turned in or as a self-assessment. Sometimes two grades may go in the grade book – the student's self-assessment using a summative rubric and the teacher's assessment using the same rubric.

The same is true for peer assessment. Students can use formative rubrics to assess the work of others. For example, when students read and critique each other's work before it is turned in, rubrics help them give specific and helpful feedback to their classmates.

For more information on self-assessment and peer assessment, see "Reporting and Documenting Student Progress" in Chapter 7.

Types of Rubrics

As the two teachers in the opening vignette discovered, the language surrounding rubrics can be overwhelming. The need for semantic clarity is critical as we examine this important piece of the assessment puzzle.

To begin with, all rubrics are **instructional** rubrics. Students learn from them. By outlining product expectations and assessing how well those expectations are met, rubrics provide students with important guidelines for improving their work. From this point on, though, rubrics can differ with regard to their function, their structure, and/or their focus.

Formative vs. Summative Rubrics

While all rubrics are instructional, and all assess student work according to a given set of criteria across a spectrum of performance levels, a rubric has one of two different functions. A **formative rubric** focuses on the strengths and weaknesses of student work and directs student growth. It operates in the nature of a critique. A **summative rubric**, on the other hand, evaluates student products and performances in order to determine a quantitative measure. This type of rubric operates as a scored rating scale.

Formative rubrics are designed to give students a better idea of where their work falls along a continuum of developmental possibilities for each of several criteria. Levels of achievement are labeled in a way that reflects developmental stages. Is this student still a Novice at this skill? Or does the work indicate that the student is operating at an Expert level? When the overall purpose of the assessment is to guide students, to help them recognize their strengths as well as their weaknesses, formative rubrics work well.

Below is an example of a formative rubric for a map project that infuses humor into an assessment process that directs as well as assesses.

MAP RUBRIC

Standards:

Name: Date:

CRITERIA		We need to talk	On the right track	Now you're there!
C R I	**Title** • Color • Size • Centered	Title lacks all the needed items: no color, size needs to be improved, not centered	Title is missing 1-2 of the needed items: color, size, centering	Title is centered, sized appropriately, and colorful
	Map Key • Organization • Readable • Colorful • Compass Rose • Details	Map key is unorganized; has 4-5 missing areas; difficult to read; lacks color; lacks compass rose; needs more details	Map key is missing 1-3 of the needed items: organization, readability, color, compass rose, details	Map key is well organized, readable, colorful, detailed, and includes a compass rose
T E	**Land Forms** • Color • Labels • Location	Landforms lack color and labels; not in the correct location	Landforms lack 1-2 of the needed items: color, labels, proper location	Landforms are appropriately colored and accurately labeled and placed in the correct locations
R I	**Cities** • Placement • Symbols • Labels 3 cities	Cities lack correct placement, symbol indication, and label; less than 3 per state	Cities lack 2 of the needed items: correct placement, symbols, labels, and 3 per state	At least 3 cities are placed correctly with accurate labels and symbols
A	**Appearance** • Neat • Legible • Clean • Colorful	Map is sloppily drawn, illegible, lacks color, and done on crumpled, lined notebook paper	Map is lacking 1-2 of the needed items: careful drawing, legibility, color, and clean white paper	Map is colorfully and legibly drawn on a clean white paper; All features are clearly labeled

Formative rubrics, in not carrying the weight of points and grades, can be far less threatening to students. They are far more likely to analyze what the rubric tells them about their work when they are not blinded by "The Grade."

These rubrics can be important sequential steps in ongoing portfolio assessment. A student can "watch" her writing skills improve, for example, as improved pieces of writing result in movement across a formative rubric from Novice Writer to Distinguished Writer.

Formative rubrics are also effective peer assessment tools. Without assigning a "score" to the evaluation, students can reflect on one another's work more constructively. The critique compliments accomplishments and gives direction for improvements.

While summative rubrics also give students an idea of where their work falls along a developmental continuum, these rubrics carry the dual purpose of also establishing some quantitative measure of the product or performance. This usually involves deriving a score from some kind of point scale which can be converted into a grade for reporting purposes.

Summative rubrics help alleviate the accountability pressure that accompanies the assessment of products and performances that do not have clear-cut right and wrong answers. The establishment of product criteria and the assignment of points to different levels of performance make communication among all parties infinitely smoother. Not only do students and parents know what to expect, but teachers are less likely to be swayed by more subjective impressions. It is easier to stay focused on the specific learning goals theoretically being addressed by the product.

On page 102 is an example of a summative rubric for a time line project. Along with the articulated, developmental stages are point values from which can be determined a quantitative measure of student performance.

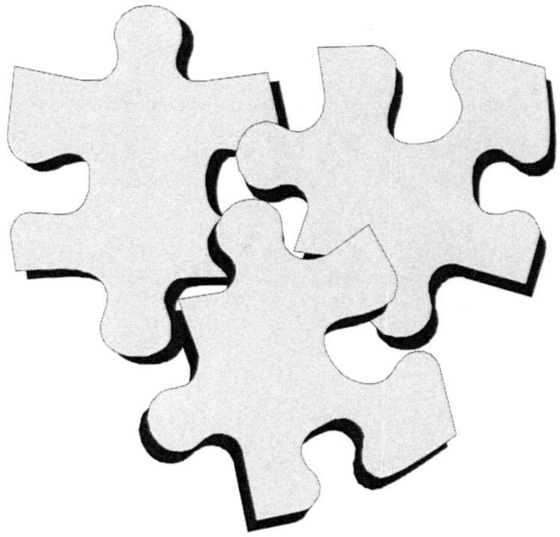

TIME LINE RUBRIC

Standards:

Name: Date:

CRITERIA	Absent 0	NSH 1	Good 2	Excellent 3	Excellent 4
Time line events	No events on timeline	Between 8 -12 events; events may not be in order	Majority of significant events listed in correct order	All significant events listed in correct order	All events creatively discussed and listed in correct order
Details on events	No details listed for any events	Names, dates, and basic definitions given for some of the events	Names, dates, and definitions show understanding of these events	Names, dates, definitions, and cause/effect relationships are explained well	Names, dates, definitions, and cause/effect relationships explained thoroughly
Time line design	Sloppy use of materials, no design plan, hard to follow	Design plan evident but visually confusing; some graphics; somewhat careless use of materials	Design plan is visually appealing and does not detract from events; neat use of materials	Use of color and graphics enhances the visual appeal of timeline; draws attention to events; neatly done	Visually creative and dramatic, design catches one's attention and focuses it on the timeline events
Grammar and spelling	More than 10 errors	7 to 10 errors	3 to 6 errors	0 to 2 errors	Flawless
Getting ready	No work done outside of class	Some notes or materials ready for class	Complete notes for entire project ready at beginning of class	Complete notes and materials for entire project ready for use in class	Complete notes, original design ideas, and all materials (including extras) ready for class
Points					
Total points				Grade	

Comments:

13 - 15	A
10 - 12	B
7 - 9	C
4 - 6	D
0 - 3	F

Holistic vs. Analytic Rubrics

While formative and summative rubrics address the function of the rubric, the terms **holistic** and **analytic** refer to the structure of the rubric.

In a **holistic rubric**, the list of performance expectations is articulated and rated for different levels of proficiency. Comparable levels of accomplishment for the different criteria are grouped together. The student then receives a single rating based on a "best fit" approach to the overall quality of his or her work.

Using the following *Solar System* holistic formative rubric, students will be ranked as Jr. Astronauts, Astronauts, or Sr. Astronauts depending on the overall quality of their posters.

Holistic rubrics look good until they are used. What happens when Fred, who can talk about his planet all afternoon, fielding questions like a NASA pro, turns in a highly creative 3-D poster that reflects his inability to spell conventionally much of the time or to construct viable sentences with predictability? Does it do Fred any good to be "demoted" to Jr. Astronaut because his writing skills are not yet up to par? Does that in any way reflect and support what Fred does know and does so well? Should his strengths or his weaknesses be highlighted by this "best fit" approach?

Because of these concerns, holistic rubrics are best used at the beginning of a project or assignment rather than as a grading tool at the end. Some students are holistic thinkers and items categorized in a holistic fashion give them a better picture of what the expectations are. For such students, an analytic rubric may initially appear choppy or confusing.

The Solar System Project
Requirements and Scoring Rubric

Design a poster to show one of the planets in our solar system.

The completed project will be evaluated as follows:

Sr. Astronaut Award

- Use of five or more colors in the drawings
- 3-D parts to the display
- Accurately labeled
- Detailed factual information included
- Additional information about the solar system included
- Most words spelled conventionally
- Writes grammatically correct sentences
- Material was memorized for presentation
- Answered questions confidently and accurately

Astronaut Award

- Three to four colors in the drawings
- Accurately labeled
- Three to four facts about planet include
- "Kid-spells" a lot of words
- Correctly uses periods and capital letters
- Information was read during presentation
- Answered many questions well

Jr. Astronaut Award

- One to two colors in the drawings
- Not all labels accurately done
- One to two facts about planet included
- "Kid-spells" many words
- Lacks periods and capital letters
- Information was read during presentation
- Answered a few questions well

Standards:

In contrast to the holistic approach, the **analytic rubric** divides and conquers. The list of product or performance criteria is set up in a grid so it can be paralleled by an articulated rating scale that clearly defines levels of proficiency. Each criterion is followed by a scale that carefully delineates performance expectations at every level. Now each criterion can be rated separately for level of proficiency.

An analytic formative rubric for Fred's solar system poster would look like the one below. Using this analytic rubric, a teacher can easily show that while Fred is functioning at a Jr. Astronaut level when it comes to his writing skills, his ability to comprehend information and his communication skills are clearly Sr. Astronaut level skills. From this assessment, Fred receives the accolades he deserves for work well done and skills well honed. At the same time, his writing deficiencies are not glossed over, but also brought to his attention. Nor, in a reversal of that, are his strengths ignored due to concerns about his weaknesses.

SOLAR SYSTEM PROJECT RUBRIC

Standards:

Name: Date:

CRITERIA	JR. ASTRONAUT	ASTRONAUT	SR. ASTRONAUT
Poster	One or two colors used	Three or four colors used	Five or more colors used; 3-D parts
Labels	Not all labels are accurate	Most labels are accurate	All labels are accurate
Content	One to two facts about planet included	Three to four facts about planet included	Detailed factual information included
Spelling	"Kid-spells" many words	"Kid-spells" a lot of words	Most words spelled conventionally
Grammar	Lacks periods and capital letters	Correctly used periods and capital letters	Writes grammatically correct sentences
The Talk	Information read from poster; answered a few questions well	Information read from poster; answered many questions well	Information memorized for presentation; answered questions confidently and accurately

Reproducible

What happens when a quantitative measure is needed for record-keeping? In the **analytic/holistic rubric**, each criterion is still broken out and rated independently of the other criteria. However, each articulated level of proficiency has been assigned a point value so that one cumulative, holistic score can be determined for the product or performance. Now Fred's Solar System Project Rubric will look like the one below.

SOLAR SYSTEM PROJECT RUBRIC

Standards:

Name: Date:

CRITERIA	JR. ASTRONAUT 1	ASTRONAUT 2	SR. ASTRONAUT 3
Poster	One or two colors used	Three or four colors used	Five or more colors used; 3-D parts
Labels	Not all labels are accurate	Most labels are accurate	All labels are accurate
Content	One to two facts about planet included	Three to four facts about planet included	Detailed factual information included
Spelling	"Kid-spells" many words	"Kid-spells" a lot of words	Most words spelled conventionally
Grammar	Lacks periods and capital letters	Correctly used periods and capital letters	Writes grammatically correct sentences
The Talk	Information read from poster; answered a few questions well	Information read from poster; answered many questions well	Information memorized for presentation; answered questions confidently and accurately
Points			
Total Points		Level/Grade	

Jr. Astronaut	6 - 8 points	A
Astronaut	9 - 14 points	B
Sr. Astronaut	15 - 18 points	C

While any analytic rubric that generates one overall rating or grade is technically an analytic/holistic rubric, in the interest of simplicity, **any rubric in which each criterion or learning standard stands alone for assessment will from this point on be referred to as an analytic rubric.**

In the *Solar System Project* example, each criterion carries the same weight in the final scoring. Analytic rubrics, however, can be weighted to favor certain criteria. See the *Travel Brochure* Rubric 2 on page 224 for an example of weighted criteria.

Complex vs. Simple Rubrics

In a perfect world where time and resources are unlimited, developing complex analytic rubrics would be a given. A **complex analytic rubric** is the completely articulated rubric with all the levels of proficiency clearly defined. Teachers would have multiple versions of these rubrics, differentiated to meet the proficiency levels of any student group. Every product and performance would have its own well-defined, structurally sound complex analytic rubric as part of an educational environment promoting authentic learning and assessment.

While this scenario is certainly one with great appeal, it is, unfortunately, not realistic. Teachers do not have unlimited time and resources. Many don't have enough time for what's on their plate already, much less to consider writing out dozens of fully articulated complex rubrics. To bridge the gap that can exist between no rubrics and complex analytic rubrics, simple analytic rubrics are an answer.

A **simple analytic rubric** has the same list of criteria as a complex analytic rubric and range of performance levels or rating scale, but the levels of proficiency for each criterion are not articulated or defined. While obviously not as precise or definitive as the complex analytic rubrics, simple analytic rubrics are a viable first step in the development of a comprehensive system of assessment rubrics.

One common practice among educators starting out with simple analytic rubrics is to define the elements of the criteria and to list those on the rubric. While still not as thorough as the complex rubric, this clearly sets product or performance expectations, and the levels of proficiency can be reasonably inferred.

What is important to recognize is that while simple analytic rubrics may be only a stepping stone to a far more comprehensive assessment system, it can be the critical first step. In order to create even simple rubrics, standards, and learning objectives must be publicly established and expectations laid out. For many students, just having that much in black and white will dramatically change how they function.

Simple analytic rubrics can be grid-like in structure (see the simple analytic rubrics in the section on Teacher-Created Rubrics) or they may be more checklist in nature. As a list of expectations on which a teacher checks which criteria have been met, what behaviors have been observed, and what elements are present in student work, checklists are simple analytic rubrics. Take a look at the *Daily Organization Checklist* on page 108, a formative simple analytic rubric.

Simple analytic checklists such as this *Daily Organization Checklist* are great tools for student self-assessment. They allow students the opportunity to examine their strengths and weaknesses concretely yet privately. From these checklists, dynamic student profiles evolve that can be revisited and reassessed as students learn and mature.

The same checklists can also be used as summative simple analytic rubrics. Point values can be assigned in a variety of ways to generate either a holistic rating for the goals on the checklist or a single quantitative score for record-keeping purposes. For example, adding points to the *Daily Organization Checklist* gives the formative line-by-line behavioral analysis a summative holistic focus. See the *Daily Organization Checklist With Points* on page 109.

The *Study Skills Assessment* checklist on page 110 goes beyond the simple "yes" or "no" of the *Daily Organization Checklist*, giving students the opportunity to rate themselves over a range of behaviors on a 1-4 scale.

DAILY ORGANIZATION CHECKLIST

Name: **Date:**

		Yes!	No
1.	Select lunch choice.		
2.	Turn in homework.		
3.	Give teacher any notes or forms.		
4.	Record assignments in notebook.		
5.	Complete journal entry.		
6.	Complete daily oral language activities.		
7.	Put materials not in use in desk.		
8.	Place materials for each subject on desk before lesson starts.		
9.	Store not completed classwork in front pocket of notebook.		
10.	Take home incomplete classwork tonight to finish.		
11.	Stack materials in desk neatly. No loose paper or materials are showing.		
12.	Place name on all assignments.		
13.	Collect assignments and place in subject file folder.		
14.	Place all books and materials needed for homework in book bag.		

DAILY ORGANIZATION CHECKLIST WITH POINTS

Name: **Date:**

		Yes!	**No**
1.	Select lunch choice.		
2.	Turn in homework.		
3.	Give teacher any notes or forms.		
4.	Record assignments in notebook.		
5.	Complete journal entry.		
6.	Complete daily oral language activities.		
7.	Put materials not in use in desk.		
8.	Place materials for each subject on desk before lesson starts.		
9.	Store incomplete classwork in front pocket of notebook.		
10.	Take home incomplete classwork tonight to finish.		
11.	Stack materials in desk neatly. No loose paper or materials are showing.		
12.	Place name on all assignments.		
13.	Collect assignments and place in subject file folder.		
14.	Place all books and materials needed for homework in book bag.		

SCORING

Count up all my **Yes!** answers.

0 - 3	Today I had some major problems being organized.
4 - 7	I was pretty well organized in some ways today but not many.
8 - 11	I was well organized in a lot of ways today, but I can still improve!
12 - 14	WOW! I had excellent organizational skills today!

Reproducible

STUDY SKILLS ASSESSMENT

Rate yourself in each of the following study skills using the scale below.

1 = I almost always do this.
2 = I use this skill most of the time.
3 = I use this skill occasionally.
4 = I almost never use this skill.

_____1. I follow written directions.

_____2. I follow oral directions.

_____3. I listen and I understand what is being said.

_____4. I take notes when I listen to a lesson or lecture.

_____5. I take notes when I read the text or other written material.

_____6. I understand the material when I do reading assignments.

_____7. I keep my belongings well organized.

_____8. I can find my assignments after I have completed them.

_____9. I manage my time well.

_____10. I plan the steps in doing long-range assignments.

_____11. I know several good memorization techniques.

_____12. I know how to preview a chapter in a textbook.

_____13. I know how to study vocabulary in any subject area.

_____14. I set short-term goals.

_____15. I set long-term goals.

_____16. I can concentrate on what I'm supposed to be studying.

_____17. I work without interruptions.

_____18. I can write an organized paragraph.

_____19. I proofread my written work.

_____20. I know how to use many different sources in research.

_____21. I use the Internet when I do research.

_____22. I take notes from many sources when I do research.

_____23. I know how to read and produce maps, charts, and graphs.

_____24. I know how to study for an objective test.

_____25. I know how to study for an essay test.

_____26. I can produce a project or product that shows what I know.

Look at the items you scored 1 or 2. Which are your strongest study skills?

Look at the items you scored 3 or 4. Which study skills need improvement?

Task-Specific vs. Unit Rubrics

> *Now that I've come up with twelve different product options from which my students can choose for their final project in our next unit, does that mean that now I also have to create twelve additional rubrics?!! — Workshop Participant*

With so much attention being directed toward developing differentiated product offerings for student expression, this question is bound to emerge. The answer depends on the purpose of the product or performance. If expertise at producing that particular product is the focus of the learning experience, then task-specific rubrics are needed. These rubrics concentrate on the elements of a singular product or activity, such as the *Map* Rubric or *Time Line* Rubric on pages 100 and 102. Such rubrics that carefully consider all the factors that determine the successful development of a specific product provide students with invaluable guidelines.

When product production is not the major focus of the experience, but the essential learning outcomes of a unit of study or lesson of instruction are, then a **unit rubric** will work best. In this case, the rubric addresses multiple tasks or items that support the essential learning outcomes. Specific products are either blended into the overall scheme of things being assessed, or they have their own line item.

The following two simple summative analytic unit rubrics are used to assess overall student performance in an Independent Study program. The *Independent Study Self-Evaluation Check/Points* (pages 112-113) is a student self-assessment tool. The parallel-structured *Independent Study Check/Points - Teacher Assessment* (pages 114-115) rubric is for teacher use. Since student product choice is a key factor in this program, keeping up with task-specific rubrics would most certainly be an overwhelming challenge.

More importantly, though, while skilled and creative product production is always a goal, it is not the essential cognitive focus or behavioral purpose of the program. These unit rubrics make evident the equal importance of every step in the whole research process from planning to production. Student and teacher assessment rubrics are shared and then discussed should major discrepancies emerge. However, since introducing these two rubrics that clearly outline performance expectations over 15 years ago, the closeness between student and teacher assessments has been astounding!

INDEPENDENT STUDY
SELF-EVALUATION CHECK/POINTS

Name: ______________________________ Date: ____________

Here's a worksheet to help you grade your work.

I will be using these same criteria to grade your work.

GRT = *great*
G = *good*
OK = *okay*
NSH = *not so hot*
N/A = *not applicable*
(does not apply to your work)

Title:	N/A	NSH	OK	G	GRT
Stage 1: Developing a Plan					
I picked a subject in which I'm really interested					
I thought of lots of topics to research					
I knew how I wanted to present my information					
Stage 2: Researching the Topic					
I found many sources of information on my topic					
I read a lot of information about my topic					
I developed spec sheets and/or notepak for notes					
I took lots of notes on my topic					
I gathered real data (surveys, interviews, experiments)					
I developed many ideas for creative writing					
I learned a lot about my topic					
Stage 3: Presenting the Information					
I organized my information well for presentation					
My final product is well written					
My final product is neatly done					
My presentation shares well what I learned					

GRT = *great* G = *good*
OK = *okay* NSH = *not so hot*
N/A = not applicable (does not apply to your work)

	N/A	NSH	OK	G	GRT
Stage 3 (continued)					
My presentation is creatively done					
My bibliography is written correctly					
I met the terms of my contract (I did what I planned)					
Time Management					
I paced my activities responsibly (I did not leave everything until the last minute)					
I used my time in class well					
I used my time at home well					
I had realistic goals for the time available					
I met the terms of my contract (I was done on time)					
Work Habits					
I worked well independently					
I knew what needed to be done and did not wait to be told					
Performance Evaluation:					
Add up the checks in each column:					
Multiply:		x1	x2	x3	x4
Total:	=	+	+	+	

Suggested grade considerations:

GRT (great) .... 76-96 .... A
G (good) .... 54-75 .... B
OK (okay) .... 32-53 C
NSH (not so hot) .... 0-31 .... D

My grade for this independent study:

INDEPENDENT STUDY CHECK/POINTS
— TEACHER ASSESSMENT —

Here are the criteria which I used to determine your grade.

Name: ______________________________

Grade level: ________ Date: ____________

GRT = *great*
G = *good*
OK = *okay*
NSH = *not so hot*
N/A = *not applicable*

Title:	**N/A**	**NSH x1**	**OK x2**	**G x3**	**GRT x4**
Stage 1: Developing a Plan					
Picked a topic of real interest					
Thought of lots of topics/ideas to research					
Developed an effective presentation plan					
Stage 2: Researching the Topic					
Found many sources of information on topic					
Read a lot of information about topic					
Developed spec sheets and/or notepak for notes					
Took/highlighted lots of notes on topic					
Gathered real data (surveys, interviews, experiments) on topic					
Developed many ideas for creative writing					
Clearly learned a lot about topic					
Stage 3: Presenting the Information					
Organized information well for presentation					
Presentation shared effectively what was learned					
Information shared was accurate					
Developed presentation components comprehensively					
Presentation was well written					
Presentation was neatly done					

Over

	N/A	NSH x1	OK x2	G x3	GRT x4	
Subtotals from Stages 1 and 2						
Stage 3 (continued) *Subtotals (p. 1)*						
Presentation was creatively done						
Bibliography was written correctly						
Met the terms of contract (did what was planned)						
Time Management						
Paced activities responsibly (did not leave everything until the last minute)						
Used time in class effectively						
Used time at home effectively						
Had realistic goals for the time available						
Met the terms of contract (was done on time)						
Work Habits						
Worked well independently						
Organized and directed own responsibilities well						
Totals						

Performance Evaluation:

Grading scale (based on weighted points, not percentages):

* _____/88 - _____/104 .... A
_____/63 - _____/ 87 .... B
_____/38 - _____/ 62 C
_____/25 - _____/ 37 .... D

* Scale adaptation for _______ N/A items.

Grade for this independent study: ____

Reproducible

Rubrics
Teacher Reflection Page

Think about rubrics you have used in your teaching. Classify them on this chart.

Formative Rubrics	
Unit	**Task-Specific**

Summative Rubrics	
Unit	**Task-Specific**

What other units of study/products/skills that you expect your students to develop would be best guided through the use of rubrics? Choose two of them and list their learning objectives in this chart.

A.	**B.**
1.	1.
2.	2.
3.	3.
4.	4.

This is the beginning of two simple analytic rubrics. You're on your way!

Chapter 9
Writing Rubrics

Well, I'd Do It if I Just Knew How

"I can't believe this," Leslie, an 11th grader, confided to her best friend. "I didn't have time to do that project for English class, so I just turned in a project I had done for history last year. I thought it might be okay since both of them were to be about the Civil War. Last year this project got a B-. Now this year my English teacher gave the same project an A. I'm happy with my grade, but it doesn't make sense. I wonder how they come up with these grades anyway?"

As the above vignette indicates, when teachers grade a student performance or product, the grade on the same product can vary greatly depending upon which teacher graded it or even upon the mood the teacher was in when the grading took place. Many teachers admit that they may grade the exact same paper differently if looking at it at different times. It is not an exaggeration to say that without specific criteria that can be used as the basis for grading or scoring a piece of student work, it is possible that grades on the same piece of work could range from **A** to **D** or **F**!

This happens because teachers differ in their views about which elements of the product are most important. If teachers themselves are unclear about what constitutes a poor, fair, good, or excellent piece of work, how are students to know what a quality product is? Students who don't understand how they will be assessed don't know what to aim for and can never be sure if they have produced a good piece of work or not. Furthermore, unless they get some very specific feedback about how to improve, they will not produce a better piece of work the next time!

Developing sets of rubrics is a complex and time-consuming task. The first step is to decide on valid and relevant criteria. Nearly all student projects, products, and performances could be assessed in a multitude of ways. It is up to the teacher to determine the essential learning outcomes for each piece of student work. Being clear on which standards are being assessed will invariably lead the teacher to decide which criteria should be used in the rubric to best show if these standards have been mastered. Make sure the criteria on your rubric matches the standards you have listed.

Pre-established product/performance criteria have been a missing link for years. How often have teachers opened exciting learning opportunities for students by allowing them to demonstrate their content knowledge through a variety of product choices, assumed the students understood the "oh-so-obvious" product expectations, and were then doomed to disappointment by uncreative dioramas, missing labels, and poorly designed brochures? Pre-establishing criteria that clearly outline expectations is a critical piece of the learning experience. It provides a focus and direction for the student, and it also gives the teacher a fair and concrete way to assess what each student does. This is the vital first step in creating effective rubrics.

Complex rubrics usually have:

- Learning standards or objectives;
- Criteria (dimensions of a product being evaluated) to be examined;
- An articulated scale of different possible points or developmental stages assigned for varying degrees of mastery, proficiency, or quality; and
- Descriptors for assessing each of the dimensions and finding the right place on the scoring scale to which a particular student's work corresponds.

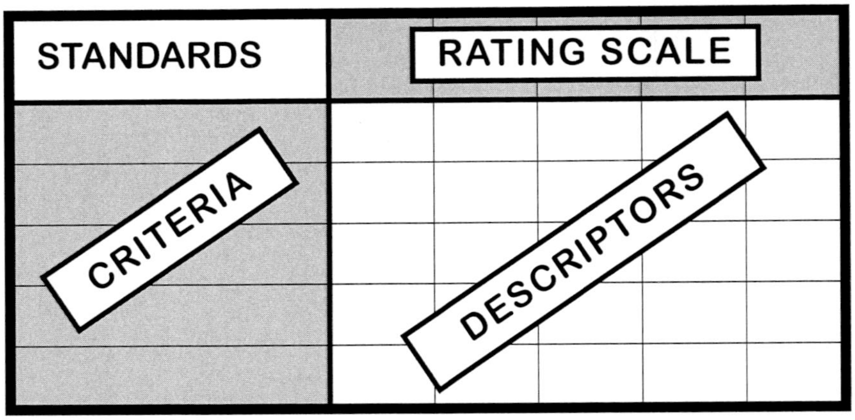

Developing Criteria

Begin writing rubrics by establishing the standards or objectives you want to assess through the project or performance. Then brainstorm all possible criteria to consider in assessing stated learning outcomes. Next, it is essential to pare that list down or to combine items in order to choose 4-5 assessment criteria for each product or performance. While there is no magic "right" number of criteria to include, too many may overwhelm students and be cumbersome for you to manage effectively.

Are there certain criteria that are consistent from one product to another, such as neatness or writing mechanics, that your district wants consistently emphasized across the curriculum? If so, develop standard criteria for those. As students recognize these recurring expectations, consistency across the curriculum in their work will follow. It is also important to reinforce the notion that certain things are always important regardless of subject matter.

One school district includes two standard criteria on its rubrics wherever and whenever it can. One has to do with writing conventions or mechanics which covers correct spelling, correct grammar and punctuation, and use of complete sentences. The other deals with appearance (or neatness) and that covers legible letter forms, effective word and letter spacing, clean corrections, and a clean paper. See the *Science Report* Rubric (p.214), the *Short Story* Rubric (p.215), and the *Composition* Rubric (p.167) for examples.

Use the form on the next page, *Criteria for Assessment of Student Products & Performances*, to record standards and/or learning outcomes and plan criteria for several of your students' products and performances.

Criteria for Assessment of Student Products & Performances

Project/Product/Performance: ______________________

Standards/Learning Outcomes: ______________________

____

Assessment criteria:

1. ______________________
2. ______________________
3. ______________________
4. ______________________

Project/Product/Performance: ______________________

Standards/Learning Outcomes: ______________________

____

Assessment criteria:

1. ______________________
2. ______________________
3. ______________________
4. ______________________

Project/Product/Performance: ______________________

Standards/Learning Outcomes: ______________________

____

Assessment criteria:

1. ______________________
2. ______________________
3. ______________________
4. ______________________

Project/Product/Performance: ______________________

Standards/Learning Outcomes: ______________________

____

Assessment criteria:

1. ______________________
2. ______________________
3. ______________________
4. ______________________

Product Criteria Cards

Offering students a variety of product options for sharing their learning is exciting and infinitely rewarding, yet can be extremely daunting as well if you anticipate having to create a different rubric for each and every type of product your students may opt to produce! Developing a set of generic product criteria cards can help alleviate this situation and streamline the rubric-writing process.

A learning task essentially has two components that need to be assessed. First and foremost, it should reflect student learning of the content material that has been studied. Secondly, there are the production elements of the product itself. For example, whether it stages a critical moment from a novel (a language arts assessment) or illustrates the steps in Egyptian mummification (a history assessment), a diorama has standard production expectations: Is it realistic? Is it well constructed? Are materials used creatively? Separating these product criteria from the content criteria makes it possible to develop a single lesson/unit rubric with interchangeable products and product criteria!

As you can see in the Inventions of the 20th Century rubric on the next page, the first three criteria focus on the important learning outcomes of the unit which all students should know. However, a student can demonstrate his or her understanding of this information through a variety of different products. This rubric is for the student who chooses to use a time line format. That student would work with this rubric and the "companion" product criteria card for a time line which would list the criteria pertinent to the creation of any time line regardless of its content focus. Here's an example of a time line criteria card:

Time Line

☐ Is there a title?

☐ Are the events in chronological order?

☐ Are important events indicated?

☐ Are time spans well-plotted?

☐ Are correct spelling & grammar used?

☐ Is it visually appealing?

INVENTIONS OF THE 20TH CENTURY

Name:

Date:

Standard:
Describe contributions men and women have made to science and technology.

CRITERIA		NSH 1	OK 2	Good 3	Excellent 4	Excellent 5
C R	10 inventions • variety of types • most important • from each decade	5 or fewer inventions are included; all are similar	6-7 inventions are included; some variety	8-9 inventions are included; variety from many decades	10 inventions are included; variety from each decade	More than 10 inventions are included; includes unique ideas or inventions
I T	Accurately listed • date for each • name of inventor	Has 5 or fewer dates and inventors OR 6-9 but 5+ are inaccurate	Has 6-9 dates and inventors and at least 6 are accurate	Has all 10 dates and inventors but 1-3 are inaccurate	All 10 dates and inventors are accurate	Has more than 10; includes extra information about the inventor
E R	Background facts	Has one fact each for 5 different inventions	Has one fact each for 6-9 inventions	Has one fact each for all 10 inventions	Has facts for each; indicates importance of each invention to the student	Has several intriguing facts for each invention
I A	Followed the **Time Line** criteria card	Meets only one of the criteria on the card	Meets only 2-3 of the criteria on the card	Meets 4-5 of the criteria on the card	Meets all of the criteria on the card	Meets all the criteria on the card with unusual detail and design
	Points					
	Total points			**Grade**		

15+	A
11-14	B
7-10	C
4 - 6	D
0 - 3	F

Comments:

Reproducible

At the same time, those students who choose PowerPoint presentations or short stories as vehicles for sharing what they learned can use the same rubric by just substituting their product choice for the time line in this example and working with the appropriate criteria card.

Another advantage of criteria cards beyond simplifying the number of rubrics you need to generate for one lesson or unit is that once these cards have been created, they can be used over and over again from lesson to lesson or unit to unit. They become a permanent classroom resource. They also provide students with a menu of options. Too often students find themselves in a product rut, doing the same things over and over again, which can lead to a numbing habituation that reduces the exhilaration of the learning process. In addition, these cards actually work as mini-formative rubrics for students as they clearly outline product expectations to be kept in mind while working.

One problem that often arises within school districts is the lack of continuity in product expectations between teachers from different grades or even ones on the same grade-level team! Use a team meeting to pinpoint those products which all students at your grade level are expected to experience or even master this year. Then quickly brainstorm 5-6 criteria for each product. Have someone type them up (use the forms on p.128) and distribute them to every teacher. Now every student in your grade level has the same product expectations regardless of which classroom he or she is in! The next step is to share them with the teaching team in the grade level just below you so they know what they are preparing their students to do and to the grade-level team just after you so they will know what they can expect from their students! This will begin to build an articulated product scope-and-sequence in your district. (See page 129).

On the following four pages are samples of a variety of teacher-generated criteria cards organized by four learning modalities—kinesthetic, technological, verbal, and visual. Printing these and ones you create on colored paper coordinated to these learning modalities will facilitate differentiating for different kinds of learners in your classroom - sometimes choices may be made from products in their comfort zones; at other times, they must choose from the other modalities.

Depending on the age of your students, how you write your criteria cards may vary. Some teachers prefer the short phrase approach as used in the samples on the following pages as they get right to the point yet have some flexibility to them as well. Others (especially with younger students) prefer the question approach used on the Time Line criteria card as it clearly demands a response from the student regarding his or her performance. For K-2 students, use full-page criteria cards with simple language and pictures that illustrate the products (see *Drawing Criteria Card* example on page 127).

Use the blank criteria card forms on page 128 to write your own set of criteria cards.

Another resource is the customizable set (88 products aligned to learning modalities) of *Product Criteria Cards* by Merritt and Coil. Pieces of Learning. Marion IL.

GAME	MOBILE
1. educational; accurate 2. challenging 3. understandable directions 4. visually appealing 5. well constructed	1. balance 2. visual appeal 3. relevant to topic 4. creative use of materials 5. well constructed
SCULPTURE	**DANCE**
1. mastery of medium 2. style 3. effectively communicates with viewer 4. visual appeal 5. well constructed	1. choreography 2. music 3. costumes 4. relevance 5. expertise
MASK	**SKIT**
1. conveys desired information/message 2. materials 3. visual appeal 4. construction 5. creativity	1. script 2. content 3. costumes 4. set design 5. production flow 6. clarity and voice projection
PUZZLE	**DIORAMA**
1. challenging 2. relevant content 3. visually engaging 4. well made 5. educational	1. realistic 2. content 3. representative materials 4. construction 5. originality 6. resources cited
MODEL	**3-D SHAPES**
1. accurate representation 2. relevance 3. neatness 4. durability 5. visual appeal 6. creative use of materials	1. correct number of shapes as assigned 2. constructs 3-dimensional models 3. discovers & records number of faces, lines, and vertices on models 4. compares & contrasts models 5. illustrates findings on a chart

Reproducible

POWERPOINT PRESENTATION

1. content
2. visual design elements
3. links
4. educational
5. relevance
6. workable animations

DIGITAL STORYTELLING

1. use of images and sounds
2. soundtrack matches visual images
3. storyboard for initial planning
4. appropriate editing
5. accurate sequence

COMPUTER GAME

1. user-friendly
2. loads and runs smoothly
3. educational
4. accurate
5. visually appealing

BLOG

1. posted on a web page
2. clearly stated writer's opinion on topic
3. has supporting evidence and facts
4. includes link to resources, pictures, or video
5. correct grammar and spelling
6. allows for comments from others

DATABASE

1. organization
2. data
3. user-friendly
4. loads and runs smoothly
5. creativity and/or originality

SPREADSHEET

1. organization
2. data
3. user-friendly
4. loads and runs smoothly
5. performs desired functions
6. originality

WEB PAGE

1. user-friendly format; all links work
2. aesthetically appealing
3. credible information
4. meaningful content; useful
5. rich, multi-leveled informational source
6. engaging

MULTIMEDIA PRESENTATION

1. variety of media
2. media competence
3. clarity
4. engaging
5. informative
6. creativity and/or originality

PHOTOGRAPHIC ESSAY

1. content
2. visual appeal
3. focused
4. balance
5. relevant
6. creativity

WIKI

1. an essential question or topic
2. more than one person contributes information
3. each person adds information and comments
4. accurate information
5. summary of the topic or discussion

NEWSPAPER ARTICLE	INTERVIEW
1. headline 2. lead sentence 3. topic sentence for each paragraph 4. 3 supporting sentences per paragraph 5. who, what, where, when, why, and how 6. spelling and grammar	1. appropriate questions 2. script 3. sequential 4. personal presentation 5. communication skills
GROUP DISCUSSION	**SPEECH**
1. regular participation 2. relevant contributions 3. respects other opinions 4. identifies problems 5. clarifies questions	1. factual content 2. flow 3. clarity/voice projection 4. eye contact 5. body language/creative dramatics 6. time
SONG	**DEBATE**
1. content 2. rhythm 3. lyrics 4. style 5. auditory appeal	1. debater provides relevant ideas 2. debater supports opinions with plausible evidence 3. debater supports with evidence from reliable sources 4. debater participates willingly & regularly
BROCHURE	**POEM**
1. content 2. organization 3. visual appeal 4. spelling and grammar 5. pictures	1. appropriate format 2. rich vocabulary 3. picturesque language 4. engaging/creative 5. spelling
SHORTSTORY	**GLOSSARY**
1. beginning, middle, and end 2. holds interest 3. spelling and grammar 4. appropriate setting 5. character development	1. comprehensive range of terms 2. accurately defined 3. alphabetical order 4. legible 5. creative presentation

CARTOON	TIME LINE
1. content 2. visual appeal 3. spelling & grammar 4. sequence 5. humor 6. originality	1. title 2. chronological 3. important events indicated 4. well-plotted time spans 5. spelling & grammar 6. visually appealing; neat
ILLUSTRATION	**GRAPH**
1. mastery of medium 2. balanced composition of values 3. balanced composition of shapes 4. craftsmanship 5. attention to detail 6. any text is legible 7. appropriate content	1. neat and legible 2. easy to understand 3. title 4. ruled measurements 5. data plotted correctly
VENN DIAGRAM	**VISUAL AID**
1. accuracy 2. compares/contrasts 3. informative 4. organization 5. legible; neat 6. visual appeal	1. content 2. creativity 3. drawing, color and/or form 4. labeling 5. spelling and grammar
MAP	**ADVERTISEMENT**
1. title 2. key/legend/compass rose 3. scale 4. content/labels 5. appearance 6. spelling	1. content 2. visual appeal/color 3. neatness 4. creativity 5. engaging 6. spelling and grammar
OUTLINE	**QUILT PATTERN**
1. appropriate title 2. main topic phrase stated and properly denoted 3. supporting detail phrases clearly stated and properly denoted 4. neatly done 5. proper spelling	1. symmetrical design 2. creative use of 4 colors 3. complementary colors 4. blend of geometric shapes 5. original design

Drawing

- Neatly done
- Clear and understandable
- Colorful
- Shows the topic well

1. ______

2. ______

3. ______

4. ______

5. ______

6. ______

☐ ______

☐ ______

☐ ______

☐ ______

☐ ______

☐ ______

 Reproducible

Using Criteria Cards: Helpful Hints

K-3

- Develop product criteria cards with your students as you introduce each product.
- Make the language on the cards simple enough that it is completely understandable to your students.
- Make your criteria cards on full sheets of paper. Include a picture of the product as well as the criteria for the product.
- Post each of the criteria cards on the wall or bulletin board for easy reference.
- You might want to color-code the cards according to categories or modalities such as Visual, Written, Hands-on, Speaking, etc.

All

- Share criteria cards among grade levels.
- Ask gifted and other high-ability students what they could add to each criteria card to make their products show additional higher-level thinking.
- Write criteria cards clearly but in a general way so that they can be used with any content or subject.
- Do a scope-and-sequence for products as you currently do for subject-area content. It is helpful to know which products students have learned how to do at a previous grade level.

Developing a Scope and Sequence for Products and Performances

For your grade level, list which products/performances:

- are introduced for the first time,
- that students know but need guidance in making/doing, and
- that students should know how to make/do independently.

Then compare your list with teachers a grade level below you and a grade level above you. From this, develop a school-wide scope and sequence of products and performances.

Student Involvement

Teachers are not the only important players in the assessment game. Students need to learn how to gauge their own performances as well. To develop their awareness involve students in establishing the standards or criteria by which their products will be judged.

Start by showing the class examples of good work and good performances that they can contrast with poor examples. Brainstorm with the students the actual elements that make one product better than the other. From these lists of elements, show the students how to pull out a list of criteria for assessment.

The chart below is an example illustrating how students have done a comparative analysis. On page 131 is a reproducible form for use with your students.

CRITERIA FOR ASSESSMENT WORKSHEET

PRODUCT: *Article for student newspaper*

ELEMENTS OF GOOD EXAMPLE	ELEMENTS OF POOR EXAMPLE
Words are spelled correctly	Many words spelled incorrectly
What it is about is understandable	Have no idea what they are trying to say
Is written in paragraph form	Is just lots of sentences with no paragraphs
Interesting to read	Boring and confusing
Can identify the main topic	Don't know what their main idea or topic is
The information is correct	Has things in it that aren't true

CRITERIA FOR ASSESSMENT

Mechanics and form

- Spelling
- Punctuation
- Paragraphs

Accuracy

- Facts are correct
- Opinions are clearly noted as opinions

Enjoyable and interesting

- You want to read it
- Some humor
- Unusual facts
- Story or examples

Clear and understandable

- Topics can be identified
- Reader can summarize what it is about

CRITERIA FOR ASSESSMENT WORKSHEET

PRODUCT: ____

ELEMENTS OF GOOD EXAMPLE	ELEMENTS OF POOR EXAMPLE

CRITERIA FOR ASSESSMENT

Reproducible

Establishing Rating Levels

The rating scale on a rubric establishes the levels of proficiency for which a student strives. Often these rating scales are simply numbered levels, with **1** usually representing the low performance end and the higher numbers indicating higher levels of proficiency. Sometimes labels like **Poor, NSH (Not So Hot), OK, Good**, and **Excellent** accompany the numbered scale giving even greater clarity to the rating scale.

Writers of formative rubrics may rely totally on labels for their rating levels since these rubrics aren't written with a quantitative summative measure in mind and therefore don't always need numbers. Humor and creativity are often apparent in these rating scale labels. Here are examples:

SETS OF RATING SCALE LABELS

Strike-out! First base Second base Third base Home run Grand slam!	Not yet Rough draft Classroom publication Local newspaper *Time* magazine	Try harder next time! In progress! You could be the guide! The Board of Education should hire you!	Novice Apprentice Practitioner Proficient Distinguished Master Expert
Minimal Adequate Commendable Exemplary	Keep trying! You're getting there! Wow! You made it!	Keep practicing! Entertaining! You're ready for radio! You're ready for TV!	Not evident Working on it Almost There Accomplished
Minimal Acceptable Awesome WOW!	Get on the road On the right track Now you're there! Wow!	The Unfocused Writer The Experimenting Writer The Engaging Writer The Extending Writer	Needs more work In progress Mastered

A general recommendation when creating a rubric is to have four steps. More than that becomes cumbersome not only to write but also to use. When there is an odd number of steps, drifting into the midpoint rating can be too tempting – not the best, not the worst, so must be in the middle somewhere. This is not always the most defining assessment. When an even number of steps is used, clearer decisions must be made near the middle of the range. A fifth step is often included in rubrics as an extension of the required work.

Writing Rubrics That Challenge

It is especially important to write rubrics that challenge high ability and gifted students. Criteria for assessment must be broad-based and demanding for these students. The challenge must be one that can be met and still be a motivator to learning something new, something with more complexity and depth. A rating scale or rubric does this by including an extension in the scale to indicate in-depth work that exceeds grade-level expectations.

Many of the rubrics included in this book have been developed with this extension in mind. On some of them, this is the 5th column on the right and is labeled **Extension.** In others, where **Excellent** spans two columns, it is again the column on the far right. See the examples on page 134.

This means that on these rubrics,
the grade-level expectations for an A
are listed in the column
<u>to the left</u>
of the Extension column.

Teachers who differentiate their expectations for students with different levels of readiness will find this extension column helpful for meeting the needs of their more capable or gifted students. The descriptors in this column should reflect more depth and greater complexity than the others. Sometimes this column has no descriptor other than a phrase such as "Over the top," "Exceed Expectations," or "Wow me!" While more credit is often given for this level of achievement, it is not necessary. When earning "extra" credit is not an option, omit the number value as the **A** has already been earned for that criterion, but recognize the achievement.

Not just the students of higher ability will benefit from the Extension column. There is always someone who gets really excited by a class project and is motivated to go the limit. How is that reflected in a rubric with a ceiling at grade-level expectations? This column is needed to support any student whose work exceeds expectations.

Standards:

RUBRIC FOR ______________

CRITERIA	1	2	3	4	5 Extension
				Grade Level "A" Expectations	Exceeds Expectations

Standards:

______________ RUBRIC

CRITERIA	Absent 0	NSH 1	Good 2	Excellent 3	4
				Grade Level "A" Expectations	Exceeds Expectations
Points					
Total points			Grade		

Developing Descriptors

The next step in writing a complex rubric is to describe verbally each of the levels of performance for each different criterion. Completed rubrics may look deceptively simple. However, finding the right language to distinguish levels of student performance is very difficult. It forces you to think about the purpose of the work and why you want the student to do it. Rubrics regularly undergo considerable readjustment after they are put to use and teachers see how they really work. It is almost impossible to write a perfect rubric, especially on first versions. However, it is possible to write great rubrics with practice and revision.

> *A graduate student who was also a first grade teacher asked me to come to her classroom and look at the spider projects her students had created. When I walked into the room, I saw over 20 different models of spiders. Each was constructed from different materials and was unique in design and approach.*
>
> *A beautifully painted gold spider immediately caught my attention. "Wow!" I exclaimed. "This one is beautiful!" The graduate student replied, "That one received the lowest grade in the class." She then pointed out a messy one made by gluing two paper plates together. "This one got full credit," she said, bringing out her rubric to share. Several elements required by the rubric were not present in the gold spider, but the paper plate spider had everything. "Do you think this is the way the grades should have turned out?" the graduate student asked.*
>
> *— College professor*

As the graduate student discovered, writing a rubric means that teachers have to think carefully and deeply about the kind of work they want from students. What does excellence look like in student products and performances? What is a mediocre piece of work?

Writing Descriptors

One way to write descriptors for rubrics is to use terminology such as **few, more, many**, and other comparative words. Be descriptive but stay away from language that may be too interpretive and subjective. This means that all the descriptors do not need to be quantitatively based (e.g., 1-2 spelling errors, 3-5 spelling errors, 6 or more spelling errors). While being that specific has its advantages, it may prove labor intensive for the evaluator who must then carefully tabulate all the errors.

Here is a generalized example of rubric descriptors:

0 = The task was not attempted, or the purpose of the task was not addressed.

1 = Minimal attempts made.

2 = Important purposes were not achieved; work needs redirection, more detail, or different strategies and approaches.

3 = For the most part, the purpose was completed.

4 = The purpose of the task was fully accomplished.

5 = The purpose of the task was fully achieved and **extended** beyond the task requirements (**exceeded** task expectations)

Notice the sequential accomplishment indicated by those descriptors—from **not**, to **most**, to **fully**, and, finally, to **exceeded**. There are many ways to show these sequential levels of achievement on rubrics. Consider these comparative descriptors when developing a new rubric:

COMPARATIVE DESCRIPTORS

Never	Sometimes	Usually	All
None	Occasionally	Frequently	Always
Poor	Part	Most	Great
Ineffective	Some	Often	Completely
Nothing	Partially	Fine	Effective
Lacks	Minimal	Very	Consistently
Inappropriately	Incomplete	Good	Outstanding
Very little	Basic	Appropriately	Exceptional
Absent	Flawed	Thorough	Extremely
Rarely	Limited	Clear	Flawless
Flat	Little	Considerable	Full
Dull	Barely	Essential	Achieved
	Inconsistently	Many	Elaborative
	Attempted	Sufficiently	Novel
	Few	Adequately	Extensive
	Vague	Competently	Superior
	Confusing	Proficiently	Superb
	Superficial	Workable	Exemplary
	Uneven	Acceptable	
	Inadequate	Satisfactory	

The best place to start writing descriptors for a rubric is to consider what students are expected to do in order to earn an **A** on their work. What are the characteristics of the exemplar, a really excellent example of the anticipated product? What are the grade-level expectations for an **A**? Consider unique or creative performances and how to indicate these features. Consider well-written, well-constructed, and/or well-produced pieces and how those accomplishments can be described.

Once the characteristics of the exemplar have been determined, the next step is to work backwards across the scale to the lowest level of achievement, carefully defining what the performance at each level will look like.

Rubrics *must* be written in language students can understand so they can be guided by them as they work. It is also very important to remember that what the rubric describes is what will drive the focus of instruction as well as what the students learn. Be sure to include everything that is important and be sure that everything you have included is important.

> *A conservative seventh grade math teacher tentatively approached me about the feasibility of having his high-ability group of students create math games. After I strongly encouraged him to do so, he proceeded with the project. A couple of weeks later, he again approached me, this time grinning from ear to ear. "It's great," he crowed. "They're having a blast. They don't want to stop. And they're doing more math every day than I could have possibly assigned. I love this!" Pleased (and relieved) that this exploration was working so well for him, I asked how he had presented the idea to his students. He promptly shared with me a very concrete, detailed rubric that clearly outlined student expectations.*
>
> *— Curriculum Facilitator*

Some teachers have asked if they should show their rubrics to their students before the work is turned in. *Of course you should!* Students should see and under-stand the rubrics *before they begin* their products or performances. When they have rubrics, not only do students have a much clearer understanding of what the teacher expects in their work, but many students find ways to improve their work even before they turn it in and before the teacher looks at it.

Grant Wiggins, an authority on assessment issues, suggests a good way to judge the quality of a rubric. He feels that if a student can score at the highest level in all of the criteria, but the product or performance is not excellent, the rubric needs to be changed. This is a good "rule of thumb" to use when creating and using rubrics.

Student Involvement

Just as they gain tremendous insight when they collaborate with their teacher to develop product and performance criteria, students of all ages will also gain insights when they participate in writing the actual performance descriptors. This is most easily accomplished when using simple analytic rubrics: the criteria have been established, the rating scale has been determined, but the descriptors are missing. First, work with students to develop descriptors for the exemplar only.

Brainstorm how the elements for an **A**-level product or performance should look. Having samples available of exceptional work may help students determine this performance level more effectively. Once the elements of the exemplar have been established, the other levels of achievement can be deduced even if they are not spelled out as concretely. If time allows, there is no reason not to expand this activity and develop a complete complex rubric with the students.

Standards:

________________________ RUBRIC

Name: **Date:**

		Absent	NSH	OK	Good	Excellent	
		0	1	2	3	4	5
CRITERIA							

> Brainstorm with the class a descriptor of the exemplar (4 level) only.

Including students in this process of rubric development opens their eyes to performance expectations. This also encourages them to take ownership in the assessment process — in the assessment of their own work. Performance standards become so much more meaningful when students better understand their goals and can internalize the vision of success.

Quantifying Rubrics

Moving from formative rubrics to summative rubrics involves simply adding points to the different performance levels. Start the scale with **0** points for the first column if the descriptors in that column reflect noncompliance with any of the criteria. However, if the descriptors in the first column reflect minimal compliance, start with a **1**.

Once points are assigned to different levels of performance, it is possible to determine a single summative score for the entire rubric. Consider the range of possible points, and assign appropriate letter grades if letter grades are needed for assessment. Some teachers prefer to assign points to all activities throughout a grading period and then determine a letter grade on the cumulative total of points. If percentages are the required form of record-keeping, determine the rubric points and applicable letter grade. Working from the letter grade, assign the appropriate percentage. If, for example, Fred earns 27 points on his project which gives him a **B+** on the rubric grading scale, his grade book percentage could be 88% (if an **A** is 90% and a **B** is 80%).

If the column to the far right is being used to reflect work that exceeds grade-level or class-level expectations, remember that an **A** needs to be aligned with the total number of points that can be generated from work that meets the performance levels described in the column to the left of an Exceeds column. This does open up the opportunity for students to earn an **A+** on their work.

Rubrics can also be weighted if there are some criteria that are more important indicators of learning outcomes to be met. This is easily done when using simple checklist-style rubrics in which different amounts of points are assigned to the criteria. A good example of this is the *Mask* Evaluation on page 188.

If students are using a complex rubric, add scoring columns on the right side for tallying points. Point values can then be weighted accordingly as this example shows:

Standards:	RUBRIC FOR________________________					
	1	2	3	4	Scoring	
CRITERIA: The more important learning outcomes are listed first and weighted					x3	
					x2	
					x1	
					Total Score	

The *Travel Brochure* Rubric 2 on p. 224 is an example of a weighted rubric.

Student Involvement

One of the beauties of rubric use is the way it lends itself to student self-assessment and comparative student/teacher assessment. Many teachers have been leery of student self-assessment, especially when it involves a grade that affects the student's overall class grade or that appears independently on the permanent school record. Rubrics with all the criteria outlined, levels of performance described, and rating scales applied shift the accountability to students. When faced with this type of well-delineated evaluation, students rise responsibly to the challenge, and teachers can be far less worried about overblown student grades.

On a form like the one below, both the student and the teacher can record their assessments of the student's work. Discrepancies can then be discussed in a conference between the student and the teacher. Using a common language to discuss expectations and performance levels increases effective communication between the student and the teacher.

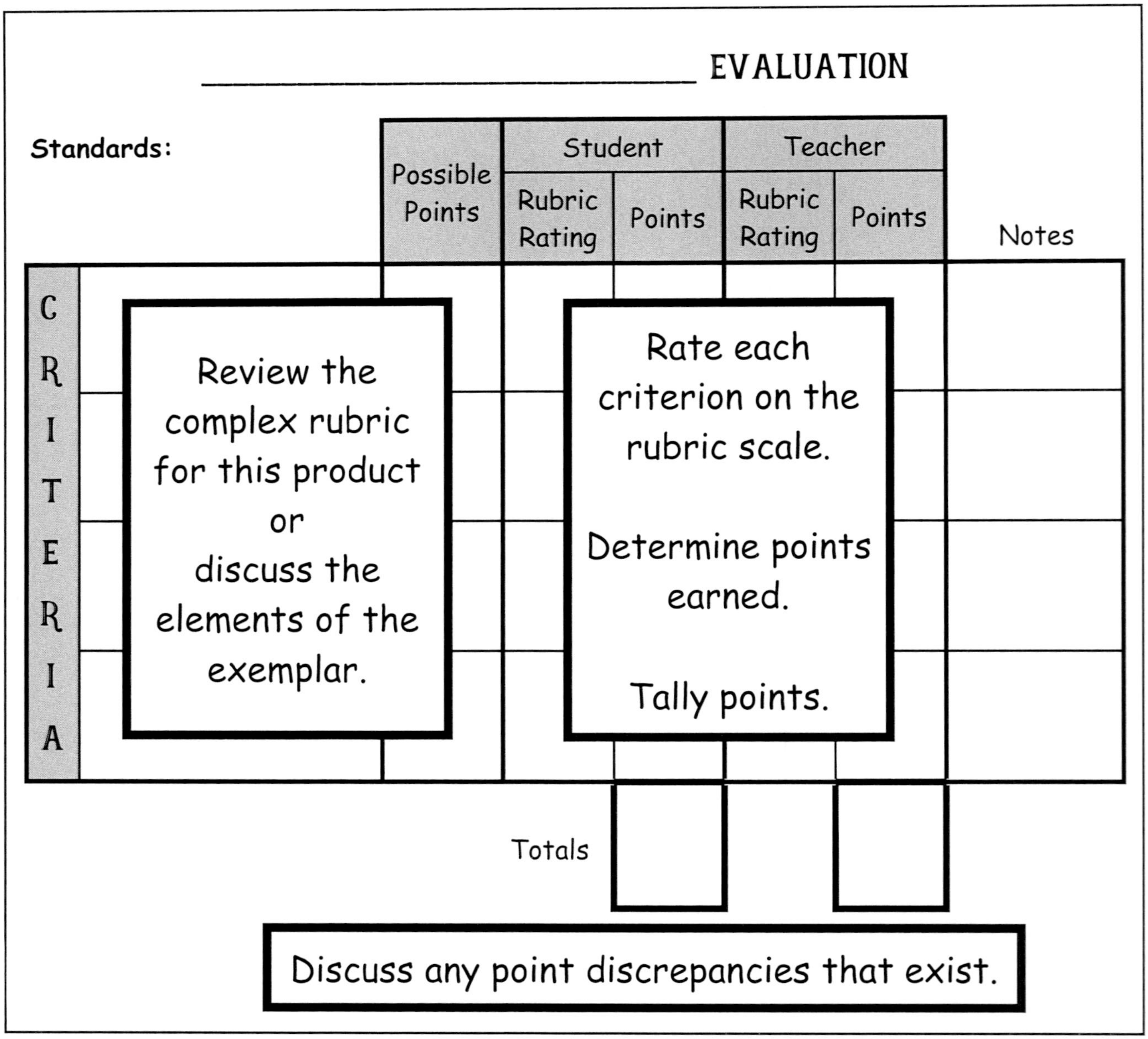

Writing Your Own Rubrics

Blank Forms

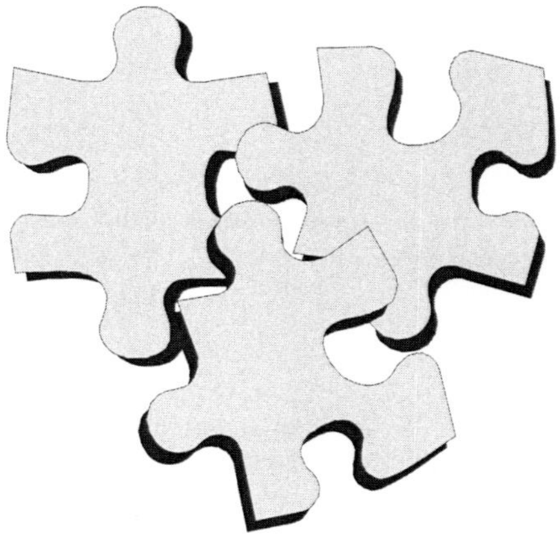

RUBRIC FOR ____________________

NAME: DATE:

Standards:					
CRITERIA					

Comments:

Reproducible

RUBRIC FOR ____________________

NAME: DATE:

Standards:				
C R I T E R I A				
Followed the [ ] criteria card	Meets only one of the criteria on the card	Meets only 2-3 of the criteria on the card	Meets 4-5 of the criteria on the card	Meets all of the criteria on the card

Comments:

Reproducible

RUBRIC FOR ________________________

Name: Date:

Standards:	Absent	NSH	OK	Good	Excellent	
C						
R						
I						
T						
E						
R						
I						
A						

Comments:

Reproducible

RUBRIC FOR ________________

Name: **Date:**

Standards:		**Absent**	**NSH**	**OK**	**Good**	**Excellent**	
C							
R							
I							
T							
E							
R							
I							
A	**Followed the** ☐ **criteria card**	Meets none of the criteria on the card	Meets only one of the criteria on the card	Meets only 2-3 of the criteria on the card	Meets 4-5 of the criteria on the card	Meets all of the criteria on the card	Meets all the criteria on the card with unusual detail and design

Comments:

Reproducible

RUBRIC FOR ____________________

NAME: DATE:

Standards:	1	2	3	4	5 Extension
CRITERIA					
Points					
Total points			Grade		

Comments:

Reproducible

RUBRIC FOR ____________

NAME: **DATE:**

Standards:		1	2	3	4	5 Extension
C R I T E R I A						
	Followed the [ ] **criteria card**	Meets only one of the criteria on the card	Meets only 2-3 of the criteria on the card	Meets 4-5 of the criteria on the card	Meets all of the criteria on the card	Meets all the criteria on the card with unusual detail and design
	Points					
	Total points			**Grade**		

Comments:

Reproducible

RUBRIC FOR ______________________

Name: Date:

Standards:	1	2	3	4	5/EXTENSION
CRITERIA					
Points					
Total points				Grade	

Standards:

RUBRIC FOR ____________________

Name: Date:

CRITERIA	1	2	3	4	5/EXTENSION
Followed the [ ] criteria card	Meets only one Of the criteria on the card	Meets only 2-3 of the criteria on the card	Meets 4-5 of the criteria on the card	Meets all of the criteria on the card	Meets all the criteria on the card with unusual detail and design
Points					
Total points				Grade	

Reproducible

RUBRIC FOR ____________

Name: Date:

Standards:	1	2	3	4	5/EXTENSION	POINTS	
CRITERIA						x __	
						x __	
						x __	
						x __	

Grade ______ Total points ______

Reproducible

Standards:

RUBRIC FOR ____________

Name: Date:

CRITERIA		1	2	3	4	5/EXTENSION	POINTS	
							X __	
							X __	
							X __	
	Followed the [ ] criteria card	Meets only one of the criteria on the card	Meets only 2-3 of the criteria on the card	Meets 4-5 of the criteria on the card	Meets all of the criteria on the card	Meets all the criteria on the card with unusual detail and design	X __	

Grade ______ **Total points** ______

Reproducible

_______________ RUBRIC

Name: Date:

Standards:		Absent	NSH	Good	Excellent	
		0	1	2	3	4
C R I T E R I A						
	Points					
	Total points			Grade		

Comments:

13 -15	A
10 -12	B
7 - 9	C
4 - 6	D
0 - 3	F

RUBRIC

____

Name: **Date:**

Standards:		NSH	OK	Good	Excellent	
		1	2	3	4	5
C R I T E R I A						
	Followed the [ ] **criteria card**	Meets only one of the criteria on the card	Meets only 2-3 of the criteria on the card	Meets 4-5 of the criteria on the card	Meets all of the criteria on the card	Meets all the criteria on the card with unusual detail and design
	Points					
	Total points			**Grade**		

Comments:

15+	A
11-14	B
7-10	C
4- 6	D
0- 3	F

Reproducible

RUBRIC FOR ____________________

Name: **Date:**

Standards:

	Absent	NSH	OK	Good	Excellent	
	0	1	2	3	4	5
C						
R						
I						
T						
E						
R						
I						
A						

Comments:

0	1	9	17	25	
	2-7	10-15	18-23	26-31	
	8	16	24	32+	
F	D	C	B	A	GRADE

Reproducible

RUBRIC FOR ________________________

Name: **Date:**

Standards:

		Absent	NSH	OK	Good	Excellent	
		0	1	2	3	4	5
C							
R							
I							
T							
E							
R							
I							
A	Followed the ______ criteria card		Meets only one of the criteria on the card	Meets only 2-3 of the criteria on the card	Meets 4-5 of the criteria on the card	Meets all of the criteria on the card	Meets all the criteria on the card with unusual detail and design

Comments:

0	1	9	17	25	
	2-7	10-15	18-23	26-31	
	8	16	24	32+	
F	D	C	B	A	GRADE

Reproducible

Chapter 10

Teacher-Created Rubrics and Other Assessments

Our thanks to teachers from all over the country
for sharing their ideas!
All rubrics and assessments are reproducible for the buyer's classroom.

ALPHABET RUBRIC

Standards:

Name: Date:

CRITERIA		Not Evident	Working On It	Almost There	Accomplished
	Identifies uppercase letters of the alphabet out of sequence	Identifies 0-5 uppercase letters of the alphabet out of sequence	Identifies 6-20 uppercase letters of the alphabet out of sequence	Identifies 21-25 uppercase letters of the alphabet out of sequence	Identifies all 26 uppercase letters of the alphabet out of sequence
	Identifies lowercase letters of the alphabet out of sequence	Identifies 0-5 lowercase letters of the alphabet out of sequence	Identifies 6-20 lowercase letters of the alphabet out of sequence	Identifies 21-25 lowercase letters of the alphabet out of sequence	Identifies all 26 lowercase letters of the alphabet out of sequence
	Identifies letter sounds of the alphabet out of sequence	Identifies 0-5 letter sounds of the alphabet out of sequence	Identifies 6-20 letter sounds of the alphabet out of sequence	Identifies 21-25 letter sounds of the alphabet out of sequence	Identifies all 26 letter sounds of the alphabet out of sequence

Comments:

ANIMAL HABITAT RUBRIC

Standards:

Name: Date:

CRITERIA	Minnow 1	Flounder 2	Tuna 3	Shark 4	Whale 5 / EXTENSION
Appearance • Neat • *Original* • *Creative* • *Colorful*	• Display is not neat, original, creative, or colorful	• Display is neat and colorful <u>but</u> not original and creative	• Display is original and creative but not neat and colorful	• Display is neat, colorful, original, and creative	• Display enhances the presentation • Display uses a wide variety of color and unusual materials
Content • Includes the animal (no plastic models) • Includes food source • Natural-looking environment	• Display does not contain the animal or food source • Environment does not look natural	• Display contains plastic animal • Food source is not properly displayed • Environment does not look natural	• Animal is original • Food source is displayed • Environment looks natural	• Animal is original and creative • Food source is displayed • Environment contains natural elements	• Animal is original and life-like • Food source is properly displayed • Environment is realistic
Construction • 3-D display • Shoebox size	• Not a 3-D shoebox-size display	• 3-D • Not shoebox-size display	• 3-D • Shoebox-size display	• Several areas displayed in the habitat • Shoebox-size display	• Shows extensive levels of the habitat • Shoebox-size display
Oral Presentation • Speaks clearly • Projects voice • Addresses audience	• Does not speak clearly, project voice, or address the audience	• Does not speak clearly or project voice • Addresses the audience	• Speaks clearly • Projects voice • Addresses the audience	• Speaks clearly with good voice projection • Focuses on audience • Maintains audience attention	• Addresses audience clearly; excellent voice projection • Demonstrates confidence • Maintains audience attention
Points					

Total points ______ **Grade** ______

Standards:

Arctic Weather Forecast Rubric

Name: Date:

CRITERIA	Zero	One	Two	Three Top of the World!	
Arctic animal facts	No researched facts about animal adaptations	4 detailed, well researched facts about one arctic animal, 3 of which relate to adaptations for winter survival	7 detailed, well researched facts about one arctic animal, 4 of which relate to adaptations for winter survival	10 detailed, well researched facts about one arctic animal, 5 of which relate to adaptations for winter survival	*You discovered the North Pole!*
Weather report	Lacks researched information about winter weather conditions in the Arctic Circle	Used teacher information to gain information about weather conditions in the Arctic Circle	Used print material to gain information about weather conditions in the Arctic Circle	Effectively used the Internet to gain detailed information about weather conditions in the Arctic Circle	*Send in your resume to the local news station!*
Illustration	No detail, no color, no labels	Illustration lacks two of the following: color, details, neatness, Arctic landscape background	Illustration lacks one of the following: title, color, details, neatness, an Arctic landscape background	Illustration has a great deal of color, details, neatness, an Arctic landscape background, and a title	*Apply to the Art Institute!*
Presentation	Could not hear, no eye contact, no expressions	Presentation lacks two of the following: volume that everyone could hear, eye contact with audience, expression in voice that made presentation interesting	Presentation lacks one of the following: volume that everyone could hear, eye contact with audience, expression in voice that made presentation interesting	Presentation has volume that everyone could hear, eye contact with audience, expression in voice that made presentation interesting	*You have a way with words!*
Points					

Your grade

Ratings

12 - 9 Keen survival skills
8 - 5 Surviving the cold
4 - 1 On thin ice

Comments:

ASSEMBLY/SPEAKER BEHAVIOR RUBRIC

Name:

Date:

Circle and tally the points.

CRITERIA		YES!	WORKING ON IT	NO
C	Sits properly in the seat during the lesson/speech/assembly	10 points	5 points	0 points
R	Stays quiet during the lesson/speech/assembly and is respectful of the speaker	10 points	5 points	0 points
I T	Keeps hands and feet to oneself during the lesson/speech/assembly	10 points	5 points	0 points
E R	Raises hands during appropriate times to answer questions during the lesson/speech/assembly. Claps at the appropriate time at the end.	10 points	5 points	0 points
I A	Knows the answer to the mystery questions by listening attentively to the lesson/speech/assembly	60 points	50 points	0 points
	Points			

Total score:

Bar Graph Rubric

NAME: DATE:

	Standard: Students will create and interpret simple tables and graphs.	1	2	3	4	5 Extension
CRITERIA	Graph Labels	No title is included and no axes are labeled.	Graph labels are present but one of the labels or the title is missing.	The graph is labeled, and the title is included with small errors in spelling or numbering.	All axes and titles are labeled and correctly numbered and spelled.	All axes and titles are labeled and correctly numbered and spelled. Graph includes a key to aid interpretation
	Graph Scale	Graph scale is not included on either axis.	Graph scale is included on one axis, but not on the other.	Graph scale is included on both axes but contains errors in increments.	Graph scale is included on both axes and all increments are correct and consistent.	Graph scale is correct and consistent on both axes. Student uses a unique scale of multiples other that 1, 2, 5, 10, or 100.
	Data Points	Data points are not displayed.	Data points are displayed, but all points are incorrectly plotted.	Data points are displayed with 3-5 points incorrectly plotted.	Data points are displayed with 1-2 points incorrectly plotted.	All data points are plotted correctly and display correct data.
	Presentation	The student's graph is disorganized and cluttered, making it difficult to understand.	The student's graph is organized correctly, but handwriting is difficult to read and bars are not drawn with straight lines.	The student's graph is organized correctly, but handwriting is difficult to read **or** bars are not drawn with straight lines.	The student's graph is organized correctly. All bars are drawn with straight lines. All labels and titles are easy to read.	The student's graph is organized correctly. The student uses MS Excel or Graph club software to type the graph.
	Points					
	Total points				Grade	

Biographical Skit Rubric

Standards:

Name: Date:

CRITERIA		1	2	3	4	5 EXTENSION
C R	**Script**	No script	Script is handwritten, illegible, and incomplete	Script is handwritten, legible, complete	Script is typed and complete	Script is typed, contains artwork, and a beautiful cover page
I T	**Biographical and Historical Information**	Biographical and historical information is incorrect	Some of the biographical and/or historical information is incorrect	Biographical and/or historical information is correct but limited in depth	Biographical and historical information is accurate, has depth, and is relevant	Biographical and historical information is accurate, relevant, inspiring, and appropriately selected for an exciting skit
E R	**Costumes, Set Design, Production**	No costumes, props, or set	Costumes not corresponding to historical period; props/set poorly made	Costumes correspond to period; props/set well constructed	Realistic costumes correspond to period; props add to the production	Costumes are beautifully selected; add realism and high interest to the production; props provide high interest
I A	**Oral Presentation**	No eye contact; unintelligible oral presentation	Limited eye contact; intelligible oral presentation but not loud enough	Eye contact made; verbal presentation is clear	Good eye contact; speaks clearly; good projection	Speaks confidently; excellent body language; engages audience
	Points					
	Total points				**Grade**	

BOARD GAME RUBRIC

Name: Date:

Standards:	Absent	NSH	OK	Good	Excellent	
	0	1	2	3	4	5
C **TITLE** • prominent, clear • summarizes theme						
R **CONTAINER** • adequate size • sturdy • thematically decorated/designed						
I **BOARD** • sturdy • uniform and adequate spaces • eye-catching, thematic design						
T **MARKERS** • adequate size • easily distinguishable • workable, sturdy						
E **DIRECTIONS** • clear, easy to follow • list materials needed						
R **CONTENT** • accurate • enhances knowledge • comprehensive						
I **CONVENTIONS** (MECHANICS) • correct spelling • correct grammar and punctuation • complete sentences						
A **APPEARANCE** (NEATNESS) • legible letter forms • effective word and letter spacing • clean corrections						

Comments:

0	1 2-7 8	9 10-15 16	17 18-23 24	25 26-31 32+	
F	D	C	B	A	GRADE

Brochure Rubric

Name: Date:

Standards:	Absent	NSH	OK	Good	Excellent	
	0	1	2	3	4	5
C **TITLE** • large, prominent, clear • catchy, concise • summarizes focus						
R **SUBTITLES** • adequate size • concise, informative • important words capitalized						
I **FRONT COVER** • title/s • eye-catching, thematic design • author						
T **BODY** • accurate data • rich details • comprehensive						
E **BACK COVER** • references listed in correct bibliographic format • contact information						
R **ILLUSTRATIONS** • enhance knowledge of topic • black ink or colored • neatly drawn and/or trimmed						
I **CONVENTIONS** (MECHANICS) • correct spelling • correct grammar and punctuation • complete sentences						
A **APPEARANCE** (NEATNESS) • legible letter forms • effective word and letter spacing • clean corrections						

Comments:

0	1 2-7 8	9 10-15 16	17 18-23 24	25 26-31 32+	
F	D	C	B	A	GRADE

Standards:

CELL PROJECT RUBRIC

Name: Date:

CRITERIA		Fair 1	Good 2	Excellent 3	Superior 4
	Describe basic cell structures	Does not show basic knowledge of cell structures (less than 4 animal parts, 6 plant parts)	Describes at least 4 animal parts and 6 plant parts	Describes at least 6 animal structures and 8 plant structures	Describes all basic cell structures (9 animal; 11 plant)
	Explain functions of cell parts	Explains less than 4 animal functions and 5 plant functions	Explains at least 4 animal functions and 5 plant functions	Explains functions of at least 6 animal cell parts and 8 plant cell parts	Explains in detail function and relationship between each cell part (9 animal; 11 plant)
	Cell model/s follows model criteria card	Has 1-2 items on the criteria card	Has 3-4 items on the criteria card	Has 5-6 items on the criteria card	Has all items on the criteria card plus outstanding use of material, creativity, and effort
	Compare/ contrast plant and animal cells	Not able to compare/ contrast	Incomplete compare/ contrast	Adequate compare/ contrast	Detailed compare/ contrast
	Points				
	Total points			Grade	

Comments:

CHILDREN'S STORY RUBRIC

Name: **Date:**

Standards:	Absent	NSH	OK	Good	Excellent	
	0	1	2	3	4	5
CRITERIA						
INTRODUCTION • good beginning • arouses interest						
BODY • develops plot • has complications, consequences, and climax						
ENDING • satisfactory; no "loose ends" • problem is open-ended and interpretative						
LANGUAGE • age-appropriate • stimulating use of vocabulary						
CHARACTERS • appropriate • developed physically and emotionally						
ILLUSTRATIONS • relate to story • colored pencil/marker; black ink • neatly drawn and/or trimmed						
CONVENTIONS (MECHANICS) • correct spelling • correct grammar and punctuation • complete sentences						
APPEARANCE (NEATNESS) • legible letter forms • effective word and letter spacing • clean corrections						

Comments:

0	1	9	17	25	
	2-7	10-15	18-23	26-31	
	8	16	24	32+	
F	D	C	B	A	GRADE

CLASSROOM BEHAVIOR RUBRIC

Student's Name: ____________________

Week of: ____________________

Parent's Signature: ____________________

Color the appropriate shape.	I did not do my best.	I did it much of the time.	WOW! I was one of the best!
I only spoke when it was my turn.	▭	♡	☆
I kept my hands and feet to myself.	▭	♡	☆
I did not disturb others during work times.	▭	♡	☆
I walked quietly and politely down the hall.	▭	♡	☆
I kept my area neat and clean.	▭	♡	☆
I was respectful and considerate of other people's feelings.	▭	♡	☆
Total	▭	♡	☆

My goal is at least ____________ Stars & Hearts.

If I succeed at my goal, I will ______________________________

____

COMPOSITION RUBRIC

Name: **Date:**

Title:	**Not Developed**	**Developing**		**Adequately Developed**	**Well Developed**	**Fully Developed**
	0	**1**	**2**	**3**	**4**	**5**
FOCUS • Issue clearly developed • Position stated and maintained • Easy to understand and follow	Focus is unclear or absent	Focus is confusing or shifts	Two or more positions without unifying statement	Bare bones; position clear; main point clear	Generally point of view is clear and maintained	All main points are specified and maintained
SUPPORT (Elaboration) • Specific statements support position • Details & examples explain statements	No support statements or details	Listing of statements or details	Some points are elaborated; list of related specific details	More points are elaborated	Most points are elaborated	All major points are elaborated with specific details
ORGANIZATION • Knowledge of paragraphing clear • Overall structure logically planned • Transition words/sentences used	No plan	Plan is attempted	Plan is noticeable, but paragraphs not done correctly	Some connection between ideas; plan is clear	Most points are connected and flow logically using various transitions	All points are connected
CONVENTIONS • Sentence structure • Spelling, usage, omissions • Capitalization • Punctuation	Many errors; cannot read	Many major errors; lots of minor errors; confusing	Some major errors; poor sentence structure	Few major and minor errors; mastery of sentence structure	Only one major error	No major errors; one or two minor errors
INTEGRATION • All parts evident • All parts equally well developed	Does not present most or all features; too short	Attempts to address assignment; confusion	Partially developed; some or one feature not developed	Essentials present	Features present but not all equal	All features evident and equally well developed
APPEARANCE • Legible letter forms • Clean, straight paper • Effective word & letter spacing • Clean corrections	Messy; out of control; extremely difficult to read	Difficult to read; some effort is apparent	Some elements show control; fairly easy to read	Most elements are under control; easy to read	Letters are correctly formed and spaced; paper is neat, clean, clear, and presentable	

(Left margin, vertical: CRITERIA)

Comments:

0	1	7	13	19	
	2-5	8-11	14-17	20-23	
	6	12	18	24+	
F	D's	C's	B's	A's	GRADE

COOPERATIVE GROUPING RUBRIC

Name: Date:

Group:		Work Harder As A Group	Keep Up The Good Work!	What A Group!!!
CRITERIA	**Job Roles**	Did not perform job responsibility	Performed job responsibility to an extent	Fully completed job responsibility
	Listening	Never	Sometimes	Always
	Focus	Off task throughout activity	Off task at times	On task
	Participation	Refused to participate	Some participation	Full participation
	Attitude	Usually negative	Frequently negative	Usually positive

Comments:

CREATIVE WRITING CHECKLIST

_______ My story has a title: ____________________________

_______ My name is on the composition.

_______ I indented the first paragraph and all the other paragraphs.

_______ My opening sentence is interesting.

_______ My story has a beginning, middle, and end.

_______ My story is well developed and organized so the reader will know what I have to say.

_______ I used descriptive words or phrases.

My two best descriptions are:

_______ I used words that appeal to my reader's sense of :
_____ smell _____ taste _____ hearing _____ sight _____ touch

_______ I included other rich details.

_______ My setting is well described.

_______ I used varied sentence patterns.

_______ Every sentence ends with a punctuation mark.

_______ Words are spelled correctly.

_______ I used three new words:__________, __________, __________

_______ My grammar construction is correctly done.

_______ I think my paper would be interesting to read.

_______ My most interesting sentence is:

Author's signature ____________________

Date ____________

CREATIVE WRITING RUBRIC

Standards:

Name: Date:

CRITERIA	1	2	3	4	5
Ideas • Relate to topic • Details	• Ideas do not relate to topic • No details	• Incomplete ideas • Few details to support ideas	• Ideas wander from topic • Details support ideas	• Ideas relate to the topic • Many details support ideas	• Original ideas and extensive details
Creativity • Creative words • Creative thoughts	• Creative words and thoughts not used	• Word choice does not evoke images • No creative description	• Words used in an appropriate manner • Creative descriptions	• Words evoke images • Creative descriptions are used	• Words enhance creative thoughts • Elaborate creative descriptions
Structure • Beginning • Middle • End	• Beginning, middle, and end not evident	• Weak beginning, middle, OR end	• Weak beginning, middle, AND end	• Strong beginning, middle, and end	• Outstanding beginning, middle, and end
Mechanics • Sentence structure • Spelling • Punctuation	• Poor sentence structure • Excessive spelling and punctuation errors	• Sentences unclear • Run-on or fragmented sentences • Serious errors in spelling and/or punctuation	• Complete sentences • Errors affect clarity of writing	• Complete sentences • Errors do not affect clarity of writing	• Complex sentences • Clearly written; easy to understand • No spelling or punctuation errors
Points					
Total points				**Grade**	

Comments:

CROSSWORD PUZZLE RUBRIC

Name: **Date:**

Standards:	Absent	NSH	OK	Good	Excellent	
	0	1	2	3	4	5
TITLE • reflects subject matter						
TOPIC • clearly maintained throughout puzzle						
WORDS • at least 20 words to be determined						
CLUES • accurate • informative • reflect research						
SPELLING • accurate						
SOLUTION • given						
BIBLIOGRAPHY • for sources of information used • correctly written						
APPEARANCE (NEATNESS) • legible letter forms • effective word & letter spacing • clean corrections						

CRITERIA

Comments:

0	1	9	17	25	
	2-7	10-15	18-23	26-31	
	8	16	24	32+	
F	D	C	B	A	GRADE

Standards:

Current Event Log Rubric

Name: Date:

CRITERIA	Fair 1	Good 2	Excellent 3	Score
Organization	Had summary of current event written on a loose paper with some of the necessary information.	Had current event in the notebook and wrote some of the information about the source but not all of it.	Put current event in notebook. Pasted in the article from the paper and included date or put the title of the TV story, date and time, name of news reporter, and channel it was on. Wrote a short summary of the article and a paragraph telling your opinion of the story.	
Included the W's	Only knew 1 or 2 of the W's. Reported on an old story.	Included at least 3 of the W's.	The summary included: Who the story was about. What it was about. When the event took place. Where it took place. Why it was in the news. It was a story that was reported within the last week.	
Location of News	Knew location of news story but could not locate it on the map.	Found location of news story on the map with difficulty.	Was able to show location of news story on the map quickly and easily.	
Story Interest	Story was not interesting or important and did not follow the week's assignment. Story was not appropriate.	Story was interesting and important but did not follow week's assignment.	Story followed week's assignment. Was interesting and important. Was appropriate.	
Oral Report	Too little practice to be able to tell the important W's of the story. Read the story. Did not appear to understand all the words, etc.	Told the story pretty well but did not tell all of the important W's. Oral presentation could have been improved with more practice.	An excellent job of telling the important W's of the story in his/her own words so everyone understood. Was easy to hear and understand.	

Comments:

11	-	15	A
8	-	10	B
5	-	7	C
3	-	4	D
0	-	2	F

Total points

Grade for Current Events this week

Standards:

DAILY WRITTEN LANGUAGE RUBRIC

Name: Date:

CRITERIA	0	5	10	15	20	25
Grammar	5 or more grammar errors	4 grammar errors	3 grammar errors	2 grammar errors	1 grammar error	0 grammar errors
Spelling	5 or more spelling errors	4 spelling errors	3 spelling errors	2 spelling errors	1 spelling error	0 spelling errors
Capitalization	5 or more capitalization errors	4 capitalization errors	3 capitalization errors	2 capitalization errors	1 capitalization error	0 capitalization errors
Punctuation	5 or more punctuation errors	4 punctuation errors	3 punctuation errors	2 punctuation errors	1 punctuation error	0 punctuation errors

Grading Scale:

100 - 71	A
89 - 80	B
79 - 71	C
70	D
Below 70	Re-do

Teacher or Student Comments:

Final Grade: ______

DEMONSTRATION SPEECH RUBRIC

Name: **Date:**

Standards:		Absent	NSH	OK	Good	Excellent	
		0	1	2	3	4	5
C	**Knowledge of topic**	none	very little understanding of topic; no facts	basic understanding apparent but confused	clear understanding of topic supported with some details	thorough understanding of topic supported with many details	exceptional understanding of topic related to other issues
R	**Organization**	none	few steps explained; not well ordered	some steps explained; order makes sense	most steps explained and orderly	all steps orderly and well explained	clear, informative steps flow smoothly and orderly
I T	**Time**	less than 1 minute	less than 2 minutes	2-3 minutes	3-4 minutes	4-5 minutes	6-10 minutes
E	**Presenter** • can be heard	not at all	very little	some of the time	most of the time	all the time	well modulated and audible at all times
R I	**Presenter** • makes eye contact	not at all	very little	some of the time	most of the time	all the time	animated and engaging use of eye contact
A	**Visual Aids**	none	very few supplies provided; not used very effectively	some supplies provided; used somewhat effectively	most supplies provided; used pretty effectively	all supplies provided; used very effectively	extremely effective and creative use of all supplies
	Points						
	Total points			**Grade**			

Comments:

0	1	6	11	16
	2-4	7-9	12-14	17-19
	5	10	15	20+
F	D	C	B	A

Descriptive Writing Rubric

Standards:

Name:

Date:

Describe a dilemma and how it was solved.	1	2	3	4	5/Extension
C R I T E R I A					
Organization • Events are listed in sequential order • Introduction and conclusion are present • Dilemma and solution are clearly presented	• Dilemma is described but there is no introduction, sequence, or conclusion	• Dilemma described • Events are out of order • Introduction and/or conclusion are not clear	• Dilemma described in sequential order • Introduction and conclusion are clear	• Dilemma described with an elaborate list of sequential events • Introduction and conclusion are clear	• Elaborate detail, an interesting introduction, and a clear conclusion • Dilemma solved in a novel way
Details • Sensory details are included • Vivid, descriptive use of words is evident	• No evidence of sensory details in description • Simple word choice	• Details include only one sensory mode • Few descriptive details	• More than one type of sensory detail is included • Some descriptive language is used	• Several sensory details are included • Vivid, descriptive use of words • Events clearly present dilemma and solution	• Exceptional use of sensory details used in novel ways • Vivid, descriptive use of words engages reader • Events present unusual dilemma/solution
Mechanics • Free of grammatical, punctuation, and spelling errors	• Multiple errors in grammar, punctuation, and spelling interfere with presentation	• Some errors in punctuation, grammar, and/or spelling interfere with presentation	• A few errors in punctuation, grammar, and/or spelling that do not interfere with presentation	• Minimal errors in surface features • Errors do not interrupt flow of the story	• No evidence of errors in spelling, grammar, and/or punctuation • Excellent variety of uses of punctuation
Fluency • Sentences are complete thoughts • Sentences have varied patterns	• Many incomplete sentences or thoughts • Sentences are not varied	• Some incomplete sentences • Some evidence of varied sentence patterns	• Most sentences are complete • Varied sentence patterns	• Smooth, natural, flowing complete sentences • Many varied sentence patterns	• Interesting novel, detailed complete sentences • Many unusual and varied sentence patterns
Points					

Total points:

Grade:

Reproducible

RUBRIC FOR A DIAGRAM

Name: **Date:**

Standards:		1	2	3	4	5 Extension
CRITERIA	**Labeling of parts**	1 part labeled correctly	2 parts labeled correctly	3-4 parts labeled neatly and correctly	5 parts labeled neatly and correctly	Labeled more than 5 parts correctly
	Originality	One dimension drawing	Three-dimensional shape drawn	Multiple 3-dimensional shapes drawn	Movable parts	Shows what the inside would look like, too
	Materials	Only used regular lead pencil	Crayons were used	Markers were used	2 different materials/ media used	Unusual mix of art media and materials
	Oral presentation	1 fact presented	2 facts presented	3 facts presented	Can identify and explain all parts	Presents extra research on topic
	Points					
	Total points			**Grade**		

Comments:

FRIENDSHIP BOOK CHECKLIST

Name: ______________________________ Date: ______________

SKILL 1: **Creative Cover**
Your cover is colorful and theme-based. ________

SKILL 2: **Table of Contents**
The table of contents is imaginative and accurately lists the contents of the book. ________

SKILL 3: **Qualities of a Good Friend**
Ten qualities of a good friend are listed in alphabetical order. Each quality is defined. ________

SKILL 4: **Photographs**
You contributed a photograph of yourself with a friend and wrote a caption for the photograph. ________

SKILL 5: **"Dear Abby" Letter/s**
Your letter describes a problem with a friend and a solution to the problem. ________

SKILL 6: **Friendship Games**
Your game includes "friendship" words. ________

SKILL 7: **Friendship Stories**
Your story describes an experience involving a friend.The story has a beginning, middle, and end.Each paragraph has a topic sentence and at least four supporting details. ________

SKILL 8: **Cooperation**
You worked well with the members of your group. You contributed ideas and helped assemble the book. You brought the necessary materials to class on time. ________

GEOMETRIC SHAPES & PATTERNS RUBRIC

Name: **Date:**

Standards:		**Not Evident**	**In Progress**	**Accomplished**	**Exceptional**
CRITERIA	**Identifies basic geometric shapes** (circle, square, rectangle, triangle, oval, and diamond)	Identifies 0-2 shapes	Identifies 3-5 shapes	Identifies all 6 shapes	Identifies other or composite shapes
	Sorts geometric shapes by attributes (shape, color, and size)	Sorts by 0-1 attributes	Sorts by 2 attributes	Sorts by 3 attributes	Sorts by more than 3 attributes
	Continues simple patterns	Unable to recognize the pattern	Recognizes and copies the pattern	Recognizes, copies, and extends the pattern	Creates a new pattern
Comments:		**Below**		**Meets**	**Exceeds**

Group Participation Rubric

Class:

Grading Key:

0 ... Never
1 ... Barely
2 ... Sometimes
3 ... Frequently
4 ... Usually
5 ... Always

Students:	Works on group goals	Asks questions for the group to consider	Supports a variety of answers w/o criticism	Shows acquisition of concepts	Applies good listening skills	Insures everyone in group understands	Total Points
1.							
2.							
3.							
4.							
5.							
6.							
7.							
8.							
9.							
10.							
11.							
12.							
13.							
14.							
15.							
16.							
17.							
18.							
19.							
20.							
21.							
22.							
23.							
24.							
25.							

RUBRIC FOR GROUP PARTICIPATION

Name: Date:

CRITERIA	ZIPPO	WEAK	OK	STRONG	WOW!!!
On task	Doing nothing	Doing a minimal amount of work	Doing some work and adding some suggestions	Doing your share of the work, adding suggestions, following directions, and not wasting time	MVP AWARD! Able to delegate work among all group members in a positive manner
Positive Comments	Being negative	Being neutral (not negative, but not praising), but listened to suggestions from others	Being positive about the activity and suggestions from other students and listening well	Being positive about the activity and suggestions from other students, listening well, and praising others	You are POSITIVELY wonderful!
Quiet Voice	Using a voice not acceptable for indoors all the time	Speaking very loudly much of the time	Speaking just a bit too loudly some of the time	Using a voice acceptable for inside group work and not disturbing the class	You are now in the Library Hall of Fame! Able to lead others to be quiet in a positive manner
Teamwork	Doing work by yourself and/or not talking to group members	Interacting very little with team members	Interacting much of the time with team members	Operating as a unified group	What a TEAM!! Encouraged members to be a group in a positive way and was fair to all members

Standards:

Historical Model Rubric

Name: Date:

CRITERIA	1	2	3	4	5
Accuracy	No/slight resemblance to original object	Attempted to make a realistic model but minimal details	Model resembles original object, but design lacks details	Good resemblance to original object; has major details	Excellent resemblance to original object; many small details
Creativity	Used only 1 kind of material to create model	Used 2 kinds of materials to create model	Used 3 or more kinds of materials to create model	Used an unusual variety of materials to create model	Created both the model and its setting using a variety of materials
Durability	Poorly built; ready to fall apart	Cannot stand alone; needs extra support	Stands alone without support	Well built; can stand alone; can be moved without falling	Well built; can stand alone; has a strong structure to support details
History of the Original	A summary paragraph copied from source	A summary with much of it copied from source	A summary with 2 accurate details written in student's own words	An accurate summary written in student's own words	A *detailed* summary written in student's own words
Points					
Total points			**Grade**		

Comments:

Standards:

How-To Speech Rubric

Name: Date:

CRITERIA	Keep practicing!	Entertaining!	You're ready for radio!	You're ready for TV!
Volume	Audience could not hear any of the speech	Audience could only hear part of the speech	Audience could hear all of speech; normal volume used throughout	Audience could hear entire speech; loud volume used throughout
Eye Contact	Read entire speech	Read almost all of the speech; looked up occasionally	Good use of note cards; great job looking at note cards and at audience	Speech was memorized; looked at audience during entire speech
Flow	Repeatedly stopped for long periods of time	Stopped occasionally to figure out words and to find place	Only stopped once during speech	Did not stop at all during speech
Speed	Spoke <u>way</u> too fast or <u>way</u> too slow; could not understand any of speech	Spoke too fast/slowly during majority of the speech	A certain part (beginning, middle, or end) of speech was too fast/slow	Consistent flow throughout entire speech
Sequence	Left out three or more steps	Left out two important steps of the sequence	Left out one important step of the sequence	All steps were included in the speech
Props	Zero props	One prop used effectively to demonstrate how-to	Two props apparent; one effectively used to demonstrate how-to	Three or more props apparent; used at least 2 to demonstrate how-to

Comments:

Rubric for HyperStudio Project

Name: **Date:**

Title:

CRITERIA		1	2	3	4	5 EXTENSION
	Content	Includes little essential information and one or two facts.	Includes some essential information with three or four facts.	Includes essential information with most sources properly cited. Includes enough elaboration to give readers an understanding of the topic.	Includes essential information with all sources properly cited. Elaborates throughout and includes details and raises questions.	Covers topic completely and in depth. Includes properly cited sources and complete information. Encourages the curiosity and the audience wants to know more.
	Buttons	No buttons move to designated cards with an effect. More than 3 buttons have problems with executing their commands.	Two buttons move to designated cards with an effect. No more than 2 buttons have a problem executing their commands.	Three buttons move to designated cards with an effect. A button has a problem executing its command.	Four buttons move to designated cards with an effect. At least three varieties of buttons are used. No buttons have problems.	All buttons move to designated cards with an effect. At least five varieties of buttons are used. No buttons have problems.
	Oral Presentation	Great difficulty communicating ideas due to poor voice projection. Little preparation or incomplete work.	Some difficulty communicating ideas due to voice projection. Some preparation evident.	Communicates ideas with proper voice projection. Adequate preparation and delivery.	Communicates ideas with enthusiasm, proper voice projection, appropriate language, and clear delivery.	Uses original approach effectively. Highly organized, well rehearsed, and used vivid precise language. Ease in delivery techniques.
	Graphics	Only hand-drawn or imported graphics used in project. Less than two tools used.	Only hand-drawn or imported graphics used in project. Two tools used.	Hand-drawn and imported graphics used effectively in project. Four tools used.	Hand-drawn and imported graphics used effectively in project. Five tools used.	Hand-drawn and imported graphics used effectively in project. Six tools used and graphics used in other printing programs added.
	Points					
	Total points				**Grade**	

Integers-Addition, Subtraction, Multiplication, Division Brochure Rubric

NAME: DATE:

Standard: Create a brochure to explain the concepts of the operations of integers	1 15 pts	2 18 pts	3 21 pts	4 24 pts	5 Extension 24-28 pts
CRITERIA — **Vocabulary**	Brochure does not include any mathematical terms related to integers	Mathematical terms used but incorrectly applied	New mathematical terms used correctly	New mathematical terms used correctly and defined clearly	Several new mathematical terms used with illustrations and examples to explain terms
Accuracy	Most mathematical facts on integers are inaccurate	At least half of the mathematical facts on integers are accurate	Most of the mathematical facts of integers are accurate	All of the mathematical facts of integers are accurate	All facts on integers are accurate. Counter examples and justification are shown to prove facts
Illustrations or Examples of Integers	No illustrations or examples graphed on number line to show operation of integers	A few examples or number lines used to show operations of integers clearly	Most examples of integers and operations are shown clearly on number line	All examples are well explained on number line and cover all four types of integers	Operations of all types of integers are shown as problems or diagrams and on the number line
Follows Brochure Criteria Card	Has one item on the Brochure Criteria Card	Has two items on the Brochure Criteria Card	Has 3-4 items on the Brochure Criteria Card	Has all 5 items on the Brochure Criteria Card	The brochure has all 5 items and is unique, exceptionally attractive and well organized
Points	All 1's = 60%	All 2's = 72%	All 3's = 84%	All 4's = 96%	100% or higher
Total Points				**Grade**	

Journal Writing Rubric

Name:

 Use a pencil. Write the date in the right corner.	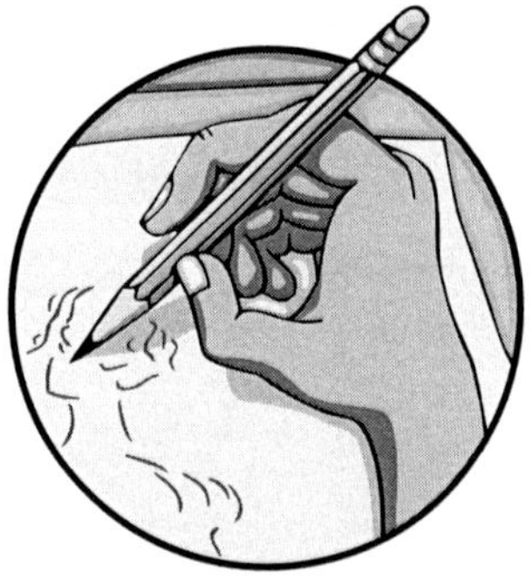 Draw and color a picture in the blank area.	 Write at least one sentence. Use a pencil and the word wall.	 Use your finger for a spacer. Use an ending mark. 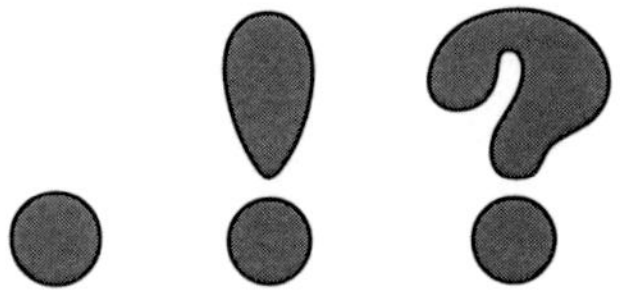	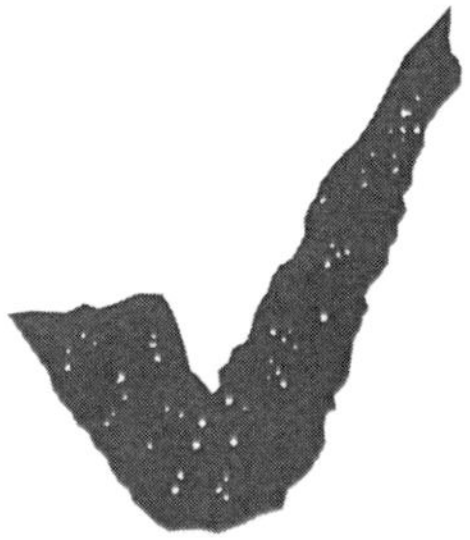 Go back and double-check each section of your rubric. If you followed directions, put a check in the box below.

If you have 5 checks on your rubric, then put a sticker on your journal page!!

Reproducible

Standards:

LEARNING RHYMES RUBRIC

Name: Date:

CRITERIA	1	2	3	4	5 Extension
Recitation	Knows 1 verse	Knows 2 verses	Knows all verses	Recites with animation and expression	Recites an original rhyme
Model Making	Construction paper and includes all characters in any order	On poster board and includes all characters in order	Creative materials, colorful, and original illustrations	In sequence original illustrations with some written words	Makes a mobile or other creative product
Vocabulary Development	Identifies 1 to 2 animal words	Identifies all animal words	Identifies all animal words and action words	Identifies all animal, action, and rhyming words	Re-writes poem replacing rhyming, action, and animal words
Dramatization	Cannot recite the entire poem	Recites with a minimum of hand motions	Recites using props, costume, and motions	Recites using props, costume, dramatic motions	Puts recitation to music or dance
Points					
Total points				**Grade**	

Comments:

MY BOOK OF LEAVES

Checklist for: ______________________________

☐ Name written correctly on name line

☐ Cover colored neatly

☐ Cover illustrated with fall illustration

☐ Appropriate color leaves on correct page

☐ Appropriate number of leaves on correct page

☐ No glue mess

Standards:

Magic Tricks Performance Rubric

Name: **Date:**

CRITERIA	1	2	3	4	5/EXTENSION
Organization • Clear statement of purpose of trick • Sequential steps in presentation • Clear conclusion	• Purpose of trick is not clear • Steps are out of order • Conclusion is not evident	• Purpose of trick is clear • Sequence of steps is out of order • Conclusion is not clear	• Purpose of trick is clearly stated • Sequence of steps is logical • Conclusion is evident	• Purpose of trick is clearly stated • Sequence of steps is elaborate and logical • Conclusion is clear	• Trick is original • Presentation is clear, logical, and elaborate • Conclusion is exciting
Props • Materials needed to perform the trick are used	• No props are included	• Props are used but some do not work or aid the presentation	• Props are used appropriately	• Props are used effectively and enhance the presentation	• Props are original, handmade, and enhance the presentation
Oral Presentation • Addresses the audience • Speaks clearly • Projects voice	• Does not address the audience, speak clearly, or project voice	• Addresses the audience, but does not speak clearly and/or project voice	• Addresses the audience • Speaks clearly • Projects voice	• Addresses the audience • Speaks clearly with projection • Maintains audience interest	• Addresses the audience clearly with excellent voice projection • Shows confidence • Involves audience
Physical Demonstration • Audience can see the process clearly • Trick is appropriately concealed • Steps of process are sequential	• Audience cannot see the process clearly • Trick is not concealed • Steps are out of order	• Audience can see the process • Trick is not concealed • Some interruption in sequence of events	• Audience can see process • Trick is properly concealed • Not all steps in process are sequential	• Audience can see process clearly • Trick is properly concealed • Steps in the process are sequential	• All criteria met • Performance is captivating, exciting, and uses creative, dramatic gestures
Points					
	Total points			**Grade**	

MASK RUBRIC

Name: ______________________ Date: ______________

Shows patterns		(15)	______
Uses several shapes		(15)	______
Shows congruence		(15)	______
Shows symmetry		(15)	______
Shows:	slides	(10)	______
	flips	(10)	______
	turns	(10)	______
Colorful		(10)	______

Total points: ______________

Grade: ______________

Math Classwork/Homework Problems Rubric

NAME: DATE:

Standard: Applies to all standards covered throughout the school year. The rubric's purpose is to provide each student with a tool to complete homework/classwork correctly.	1	2	3	4	5 Extension
CRITERIA — Computation of mathematics problems	Fewer than 50% of the computations are correct.	Includes correct computations on 50% - 74% of problems.	Includes correct computations 75% - 99% of the problems.	Includes correct computations of all problems.	Everything in #4 and shows multiple computational approaches.
Approach to the problems	Unable to generate any strategies to solve problems	Begins, however fails to complete problems	Begins, but doesn't finish or leaves out important parts of the solution.	Clear organized method. All solutions are correct and work shown.	Everything in #4 and the methods used can stand alone.
Written Explanation	Explanation is non-existent	Explanation is incomplete	Explanation is correct but basic with few details	Clear, sequential, detailed explanation	Everything in #4 plus all mathematical terms are used
Understanding of problems	Demonstrates no understanding of problem	Minimal understanding of the problem	Understands the problem and what is being asked	Excellent understanding of the problem with complete thoughts	Everything in #4 and shows/explains more than the problem asks
Points					
Total points				Grade	

Math Vocabulary Crossword Puzzle Rubric

Standard: Understands terminology for mathematical concepts	NAME: 1 15 pts	2 18 pts	DATE: 3 21 pts	4 24 pts	5 Extension 24-28 pts
Vocabulary	Clues for 0-4 vocabulary words across and 0-4 vocabulary words down are included.	Clues for 5-9 vocabulary words across and 5-9 vocabulary words down are included	Clues for 10-14 vocabulary words across and 10-14 vocabulary words down are included.	Clues for 15-19 vocabulary words across and 15-19 vocabulary words down are included.	Clues for 20 or more vocabulary words across and 20 or more vocabulary words down are included.
Content	Clues did not come from Math definitions, concepts, rules. postulates, or ideas	Missing information come from Math definitions, concepts, rules, postulates, concepts, or ideas	Has many errors with information come from Math definitions, concepts, rules, postulates, concepts, or ideas	Most information is accurate dome from Math definitions, concepts, rules, postulates, concepts, or ideas	Has accurate, complete information come from Math definitions, concepts, rules, postulates, concepts or ideas
Neatness	The work appears sloppy and unorganized. It is hard to know what information goes together.	The work is presented in an organized fashion but may be hard to read at time	The work is presented in a neat and organized fashion that is usually easy to read	The work is presented in a neat, clear. organized fashion that is very easy to read	Spectacular use and organization of space. The clues are legible.
Mathematical Terminology	Math Terminologies used show very limited understanding of the underlying concepts	Math Terminologies show some understanding of the mathematical concepts	Math Terminologies show substantial understanding of the mathematical concepts	Math Terminologies show complete understanding of the mathematical concepts	Math Terminologies show extensive understanding of the mathematical concepts
Points	All 1's = 60%	All 2's = 72%	All 3's = 84%	All 4's = 96%	100% or higher
Total Points				**Grade**	

CRITERIA

Mathematical Problem Solving Rubric

Standards:

Name: Date:

CRITERIA	1	2	3	4	5/EXTENSION
Conceptual Understanding	Shows no understanding of the problem's mathematical concepts and principles	Shows very limited understanding of the problem's mathematical concepts and principles; makes major computational errors	Shows understanding of some of the problem's mathematical concepts and principles; may contain serious computational errors	Shows nearly complete understanding of the problem's mathematical concepts and principles; uses nearly correct mathematical terminology and notations; executes algorithms completely; computations are generally correct but may contain minor errors	Shows understanding of the problem's mathematical concepts and principles; uses appropriate mathematical terminology and notations; executes algorithms completely and correctly
Procedural Knowledge	Attempts to use irrelevant outside information; fails to indicate which elements of the problem are appropriate; copies part of the problem, but without attempting a solution	Attempts to use irrelevant outside information; fails to identify important elements; inappropriate strategy for solving the problem; solution process is missing or difficult to identify	Identifies some important elements of the problems, but shows only limited understanding of the relationships between them; solution process is incomplete	Identifies the most important elements of the problems and shows general understanding of the relationships between them; solution process is nearly complete	Uses relevant outside information of a formal or informal nature; identifies all the important elements of the problem and shows understanding of the relationships between them; gives clear evidence of a solution process; solution process is complete and systematic
Communication	Communicates ineffectively; words do not reflect the problem; may include drawings which completely misrepresent the problem situation	Has some satisfactory elements but may fail to complete or may omit significant parts of the problem; explanation or description may be missing or difficult to follow; diagram is unclear and difficult to interpret	Makes significant progress towards completion of the problem; explanation or description is unclear	Gives a fairly complete response with reasonable clear explanations or descriptions; includes a nearly complete appropriate diagram; communicates effectively to the identified audience	Gives a complete response with clear, coherent, and elegant explanations; strong supporting arguments which are logically sound and complete; includes examples and counter-examples
Points					
Total points				**Grade**	

MONEY RUBRIC

Name: Date:

Standards:

		1 Point	2 Points	3 Points
CRITERIA	Identifying coins	Does not recognize coins	Recognizes a penny, nickel, dime	Recognizes a penny, nickel, dime, quarter, half dollar
	Counting money	Does not count coins accurately	Counts coins accurately yet unable to count higher than a dollar	Counts coins accurately and counts up to five dollars or higher
	Making change	Unable to make change	Makes change for amounts under a dollar	Makes change for amounts up to five dollars or higher

Comments:

SCORING

Points	Description
9	Exceeds Expectation
7 — 8	Excellent
5 — 6	Satisfactory
3 — 4	Needs Improvement

NEWSPAPER RUBRIC

Name: **Date:**

Standards:	Absent	NSH	OK	Good	Excellent	
	0	1	2	3	4	5
VISUAL FORMAT • effective arrangement of parts — articles, photos, ads • column-style arrangement • logo						
FORMAT OF ARTICLES • headlines — relate to key words in article • introduction — topic sentence • body — who, what, why, where, when						
CONTENT • variety of articles • variety of ads • photos, illustrations, and graphics appropriate to purpose						
CONVENTIONS (MECHANICS) • correct spelling • correct grammar and punctuation • complete sentences						
APPEARANCE (NEATNESS) • legible letter forms • effective word and letter spacing • clean corrections						

CRITERIA

Comments:

0	1 2-7 5	6 7-9 10	11 12-14 15	16 17-19 20+	
F	D	C	B	A	GRADE

NUMBER SENSE RUBRIC

Standards:

Name: Date:

This student can:

CRITERIA		Needs More Work	In Progress	Mastered
C	Identify *equal* groups			
R	Compare groups: identify *more*			
I	Compare groups: identify *less*			
T	Identify the *number of objects* in a group 1-10 and record it			
E	Show the number that is *one more* or *one less*			
R	*Label groups* of objects 1-10			
I	*Order groups* of objects by number			
A	Identify a *missing number* in a sequence			

Standards:

OPTICAL ILLUSIONS BOOKLET RUBRIC

Name: Date:

CRITERIA		1	2	3	4	5/EXTENSION
C R I	**Drawings represent optical illusions** • Traditional • Original	• Optical illusions are not evident	• Traditional illusions included • Original illusion is not clear	• Traditional illusions included and clear • Most original illusions are identifiable	• Several examples of traditional illusions included • Original illusions are all clear	• Optical illusions are detailed and varied • Exceptional use of original ideas
T	**Questions about and answers to optical illusions address the features to be identified**	• Questions and/or answers are not included	• Questions and/or answers are presented for most illusions but some are not related	• Most questions and/or answers are included and related	• Questions and answers are there for all illusions • Questions present a challenge • Questions and answers are related	• Excellent, thought-provoking questions and surprising, original answers for all optical illusions
E R I	**Organization** • Table of Contents • Explanation of nature of illusions • Numbered pages • Questions on pages • Answers in index	• Booklet is not organized • Missing organization criteria	• Booklet is organized • Missing one or more parts	• Booklet is organized • All criteria included	• Booklet is organized • All criteria included • Several examples of illusions included	• Booklet is organized • All criteria included • Many varied and unusual optical illusions included
A	**Neatness** • Optical illusions • Text	• Drawings and text are not legible	• Drawings and text are legible but not neat	• Drawings and text are neat, legible, but not centered	• Drawings and text are neat, legible, and centered	• Drawings are legible and neat • Text is typed and centered
	Points					

Total points ______ **Grade** ______

ORAL PRESENTATION RUBRIC

Standards:

Name: Date:

CRITERIA	1	2	3	4	5
Organization	Audience cannot understand presentation because there is no sequence of information.	Student presents information in a sequence which audience can barely follow.	Student presents information in a logical sequence which audience can follow some of the time.	Student presents information in a logical sequence which audience can follow most of the time.	Student presents information in logical, interesting sequence which audience can follow all of the time.
Eye Contact	Student reads all of report with no eye contact.	Student occasionally uses eye contact, but still reads most of report.	Student uses eye contact some of the time, but still returns to notes.	Student maintains eye contact almost all of the time but returns to notes one time.	Student maintains eye contact all of the time with audience and never returns to notes.
Graphics	Graphics rarely relate to text and presentation.	Graphics relate to text and presentation in an adequate manner.	Graphics relate to text and presentation in a competent manner.	Graphics relate to text and presentation in a proficient manner.	Graphics explained and reinforce text and presentation in an exceptional manner.
Subject Knowledge	Student has very little knowledge of the Information and cannot answer questions about subject.	Student is not comfortable with information and is able to answer only rudimentary questions.	Student is at ease with expected answers to some of the questions, but fails to elaborate.	Student is at ease with expected answers to most of the questions and elaborates.	Student demonstrates full knowledge by answering all class questions with explanations and elaboration.
Points					
Total points				**Grade**	

Standards:

ORIGAMI RUBRIC

Name: Date:

CRITERIA		1	2	3	4	5/EXTENSION
	Construction	• Product is poorly constructed • Careless folds • Shoddy design	• Product is constructed • Design flaws are evident	• Product is constructed • Fold lines are neat • Not all fold lines are crisp	• Product fits together well • Fold lines are neat and crisp	• Product is perfectly constructed • Symmetrical design is flawless • Crisp, clean folds
	Materials • quality • types	• No paper origami product	• Constructed with paper, but not origami-type paper	• Use origami paper • Also uses glue, tape, staples	• Uses origami paper, generally of high quality	• Uses high quality paper of differing colors to emphasize contrasts in product
	Design • creativity • uniqueness	• No product • • Product was pre-fabricated	• Has product • Not constructed using origami principles	• Product constructed using origami principles	• Interesting origami design • Creative design from challenging origami book	• Product is "one-of-a-kind" • Imaginative design • Creative design not found in any book
	Verbal Explanation	• No eye contact • No verbal presentation	• Limited eye contact • Verbal presentation cannot be heard by audience	• Eye contact made • Verbal presentation is clear	• Good eye contact • Speaks clearly • Projects voice well • Acknowledges audience	• Outstanding body language/eye contact • Confidently addresses audience • Engages audience
	Points					
		Total points			**Grade**	

PAMPHLET RUBRIC

Name: Date:

Standards:

CRITERIA		Absent 0	NSH 1	OK 2	Good 3	Excellent 4	Excellent 5
ORGANIZATION	• follows Table of Contents						
CONTENT	• contains all required sections						
	• contains appropriate additional sections						
	• presents accurate information						
WRITTEN PARTS	• written in your own words						
	• uses correct capitalization, punctuation, and grammar						
	• accurate spelling						
VISUAL APPEAL	• uses easy-to-read labeled charts, graphs, and/or illustrations						
	• has balance — equal amount of written and illustrative material						
	• is neatly done — legible and clean						
BIBLIOGRAPHY	• lists a variety of sources						
	• correctly written						
CREATIVITY	• shows originality in design • uses elaborative details						

Comments:

0	1-3	14-16	27-29	40-42	
	4-10	17-23	30-36	43-50	
	11-13	24-26	37-39	51+	
F	D	C	B	A	GRADE

 Reproducible

Personal Process Rubric

Student ______________________________ **Date** ____________

Project or Unit: ______________________________

WORK HABITS	**Frequently**	**Sometimes**	**Not Yet**
• Work done on time	______	______	______
• Use good organizational skills	______	______	______
• Make use of reference materials	______	______	______
• Involve reading and math skills	______	______	______
• Use time well	______	______	______
• Take initiative	______	______	______
• Ask for help when needed	______	______	______

WORKING WITH OTHERS	**Frequently**	**Sometimes**	**Not Yet**
• Work well with others	______	______	______
• Have good listening skills	______	______	______
• Solve conflicts in a positive manner	______	______	______
• Show leadership skills	______	______	______
• Assist others	______	______	______

(YOUR CATEGORY) ____________________	**Frequently**	**Sometimes**	**Not Yet**
•	______	______	______
•	______	______	______
•	______	______	______
•	______	______	______

Persuasive Essay Rubric

Name: Date:

Standards:		Whatever!	Yeah, maybe?	I'm convinced!	I'll do whatever you want me to do!!!	
		1	2	3	4	Score
CRITERIA	Content (claim and support)	The argument or claim is not mentioned; no reasons are given to support the claim; no reasons are given against the claim	The claim is confused or unclear; 1 or 2 weak reasons, irrelevant reasons, or confusing reasons; no argument against the claim is mentioned	The claim is made; reasons are given in support of the claim but important reasons are overlooked; no arguments against the claim are mentioned	The claim is made; clear accurate reasons support the claim; arguments against the claim are discussed and proven insignificant	
	Organization	The writing is very disorganized and often off topic	The writing is workable but sometimes is off topic	The writing has a clear beginning, middle, and end	The essay has a compelling opening, a fully developed body, and a conclusion that calls for action	
	Sentence Fluency	So many run-ons and fragments make the piece difficult to read	A few of the sentences contain run-ons, fragments, or are awkward to read	The sentences are well constructed but do not vary	The sentences are clear, complete, and of varying lengths and types	
	Mechanics	Mistakes in spelling, usage, and punctuation detract from the clarity and meaning	Mistakes in spelling, usage, and punctuation are few but do not detract significantly from the piece	There are no mistakes in spelling, usage, or punctuation	Not only are there no mistakes but the writer is inventive in his/her use of mechanics	

Comments:

Total points

Grade

Reproducible

Persuasive Speech Rubric

Standards:

Name: Date:

CRITERIA	1	2	3	4	5
Organization	Attempted but not written as a speech.	Speech included topic sentence and detail. Sentences did not give support.	Speech included topic sentence with at least one detail sentence.	Speech included topic sentences with two detail sentences.	Speech included topic sentence with 3 or more details in logical order. Flowed well.
Content	Attempts to give purpose/importance only for the speech.	Gives purpose/importance but reasons are unclear. Not persuasive.	Describes the purpose/importance with only one reason in a persuasive way.	Clearly states the purpose/importance with 2 reasons in a persuasive way.	Clearly states purpose/importance with 3 or more reasons in a persuasive way.
Grammar	Speech is unreadable due to grammatical errors.	Speech is difficult to understand due to grammatical errors.	Speech given with several grammatical errors.	Speech given with minimal grammatical errors.	Speech given with correct grammar.
Oral Presentation	Speech read directly from the paper.	Speech read with little eye contact.	Speech presented with eye contact and voice inflection.	Speech presented with voice inflection, sincerity, and minimal gestures.	Speech presented with voice inflection, sincerity, emotions, and gestures given.
Points					
Total points				**Grade**	

Comments:

Picture Essay Rubric

Standards:

Name: Date:

CRITERIA	1	2	3	4	5/EXTENSION
Picture accurately illustrates different elements of topic	• No evidence of accurate research	• Includes some examples accurately but not all elements are represented	• Includes at least one example of each element accurately	• Includes several examples of each element • Shows a cohesive relationship between elements	• Picture essay is an accurate depiction of the topic • All elements are interrelated and illustrated in detail
Labels • **Included** • **Provide additional information about topic**	• No labels are included	• Some labels are included but do not provide background information	• Labels are clear, accurate, and included for most items	• Labels are clear, descriptive, and contribute to an understanding of the topic	• All items are labeled • Labels are detailed, neat, descriptive, and contribute to an understanding of topic
Neatness	• Difficult to discriminate features • Reading labels is difficult	• Some pictures and labels are neatly done	• Most pictures and labels are neatly done	• All pictures and labels are neatly done	• Excellent, clear, and detailed drawings • Labels are neat and may be typed
Presentation to class • **Explanation of details in picture is clear** • **All elements of topic are identified**	• Picture essay is not presented	• Picture essay is presented with little attention to details	• Picture essay is presented • Different elements of topic are clearly introduced	• Presentation effectively and accurately introduces the topic • Accurate details are shared	• Presentation engages the audience and keeps their interest • Knowledge of topic is illustrated by accuracy of answers to questions
Points					
	Total points			**Grade**	

RUBRIC FOR PIONEER TOOLS

Standard:

The student will understand how tools helped pioneers settle the land.

Name: Date:

CRITERIA	1	2	3	4	5/EXTENSION
Accurate model of tool that shows how it was used during pioneer life between 1800-1850	Has a model of tool, but it is not historically accurate and does not relate to pioneer life	Has item accurate for time period but does not show historical setting	Has item accurate for time period and shows relationship to pioneers in an historical setting	All of 3, plus shows item in an historically accurate scene being used by a pioneer	Includes all of 4 plus shows historical person using item
Informational index card with historical background of the tool that also describes how it was used	Card has only title or name of tool, but no other information	Has card, but information does not relate to the model or is not historically accurate	Has correct information related to the tool and the setting, but has few details	Information on card is detailed and clearly shows connection between the tool and pioneer life	All of 4 plus shows connection between items, historical setting, and person who lived between 1800-1850
Followed the Model criteria card	Meets only one of the items on the criteria card	Meets only 2-3 of the items on the criteria card	Meets 4-5 of the items on the criteria card	Meets all of the items on the criteria card	Meets all the items on the criteria card with unusual detail and design
Points					
Total points				**Grade**	

Play Rubric

Name: **Date:**

Standards:		Absent	NSH	OK	Good	Excellent	
		0	1	2	3	4	5
C	**CHARACTERS** • appropriate • developed physically & emotionally						
R	**SETTING** • well established • appropriate for staging						
I	**PLOT** • clear statement of problem • rising action to climax • effective climax • satisfactory conclusion						
T	**DIALOGUE** • realistic						
E	**INTEGRATION** • all parts evident • all parts well developed						
R	**SCRIPT** • proper format • correct spelling • correct punctuation & capitalization						
I	**APPEARANCE** • legible letter forms • clean, straight paper • effective word & letter spacing • clean corrections						
A	**PERFORMANCE** • clear presentation of dialogue • effectively staged • creative costuming & props						

Comments:

0	1	9	17	25	
	2-7	10-15	18-23	26-31	
	8	16	24	32+	
F	D	C	B	A	GRADE

 Reproducible

Rubric for Poetry Book

Name:

Date turned in:

Standards:	Poor 1	Fair 2	Great 3	Excellent 4	Score
Organization	• Shows very little organization or is missing page numbers or table of contents.	• Hard to recognize organizational plan • 10 poems • Table of Contents or page numbers not easy to follow	• Pretty well organized • 10 poems • 5 illustrations • Cover • Table of Contents • Pages numbered	• Very well organized • Follows a clear theme or plan • Effective cover • Table of Contents • 10 poems • 5 illustrations • Pages numbered	
Content • simile • metaphor • ballad • personification • haiku • onomatopoeia • 4-line rhyme • alliteration • repetition	• Lacking required number of poems or illustrations • Shows that little time spent trying to fulfill requirements	• 10 poems • Missing the variety of forms that were required • Needs a little work understanding some of the forms	• 10 poems • Understands most of the different forms of poetry • Pretty good at using poetry to express ideas	• Includes all the required forms • Clearly understands the different types of poetry • Can use poetry effectively to express himself/herself	
Illustrations	• Lacking required number of illustrations • Not original	• 5 illustrations • Do not reflect much effort	• 5 original illustrations • Well done • Hard to see how some relate to poems	• Original illustrations on at least 5 poems and on cover • Chosen to complement meaning of poems	
Creativity	• Lacks creativity • Little attempt to be original • "Borrowed" ideas	• Attempt made to be creative • Some ideas were just variations on other poems	• Pretty creative • Some original ideas	• Clearly shows a great deal of creativity • Expresses original ideas or ideas in an original way	
Mechanics	• Contains a lot of grammatical or spelling errors • Needs quite a bit of revising	• Contains some grammatical and/or spelling errors	• Contains a few grammatical and/or spelling errors	• Titled poems • No grammar, spelling, or punctuation errors	
Appearance	• Written on notebook paper • Quite messy	• Typed or written on unlined paper • Messy	• Typed or written neatly on unlined paper	• Typed or written neatly on unlined paper • Quality work	

(Left side label: CRITERIA)

Comments:

17 - 20	A
13 - 16	B
9 - 12	C
5 - 8	D
4 or less	F

Total points

Grade

Poetry Project Checklist

1. I read this book of poetry: ______________________________

2. I memorized this poem: ______________________________

____ 3. I have practiced reciting it and am ready to recite it to the class.

____ 4. I made an attractive cover for my poetry book.

5. I wrote at least 10 original poems. I have included:

    ______ simile
    ______ metaphor
    ______ personification
    ______ onomatopoeia
    ______ haiku
    ______ ballad
    ______ 4-line rhyme
    ______ alliteration
    ______ repetition

6. I typed the poems or wrote them in my best handwriting on unlined paper.

____ 7. I gave each poem a title.

____ 8. I included a table of contents.

9. I numbered each page.

10. I included an appropriate, original illustration with at least 5 of the poems.

____ 11. My poetry project was done neatly.

____

My signature ______________________________

Date ________________

POETRY RUBRIC

Name: **Date:**

Standards:	Absent	NSH	OK	Good	Excellent	
	0	1	2	3	4	5
C R I T E R I A						
SUBJECT • appropriate • developed; shows depth						
WORDING • interesting use of words • well chosen vocabulary • meaningful to subject						
FORMAT • words and ideas arranged according to accepted poetic structure						
ILLUSTRATIONS (optional) • appropriate to content						
CONVENTIONS (MECHANICS) • correct spelling • correct grammar • correct punctuation						
APPEARANCE (NEATNESS) • legible letter forms • effective word and letter spacing • clean corrections • borrowed illustrations neatly trimmed						

Comments:

0	1 2-4 5	6 7-9 10	11 12-14 15	16 17-19 20+	
F	D	C	B	A	GRADE

Position Paper Rubric

Standards:

Name: Date:

Criteria	1	2	3	4	5/Extension
Understanding	Demonstrates basic knowledge of position	Shows impact of position on other elements	Adequately demonstrates the perception of position	Questions the validity of history's depiction of position	Develops independently a theory based in fact confirming or denying position
Resources	Relies solely on what is heard in class	Uses one encyclopedia article or internet "blurb" in addition to class information	Uses three independent sources of information	Independently pursues volume/s listed in a bibliography	Contacts a university to find further information
Organization	Use of introductory paragraph to list discussion topics in paper	Use of sequential discussion based on information presented in introductory paragraph	Discussion within each paragraph in logical order as implied by introductory paragraph	Paper successfully defends its thesis and has a logical conclusion	Thesis leads student and/or instructor to a new level of research on position
Clarity of Thought	Concrete statements only of facts (no analysis)	Very basic analysis of facts (e.g., use of "I think')	Basic abstract reasoning applied to facts; written in third person	Facts become the skeleton upon which reasoned analysis is placed	Reasoning is so complete and precisely stated that it seems obvious and is easily understood
Points					

Total points ______ **Grade** ______

POSTER RUBRIC

Name: **Date:**

Standards:

CRITERIA	Absent	NSH	OK	Good	Excellent	
	0	1	2	3	4	5
TITLE • largest print • legible, uniform letters • concise, summarizes theme						
GRAPHICS • highlight key concepts • arrangement leads visual direction • appropriately sized • properly trimmed if borrowed						
NEGATIVE SPACE • surrounds text, graphics, and boundary of product effectively						
BACKGROUND • non-obtrusive						
LABELS • smaller than title • legible, uniform letters • clearly identify object						
TEXT • used as necessary • accurate spelling and punctuation						
RESOURCES • for sources of information used • correctly written • visible yet discreet						
APPEARANCE (NEATNESS) • legible letter forms • effective word and letter spacing • clean corrections						

Comments:

0	1	9	17	25	
	2-7	10-15	18-23	26-31	
	8	16	24	32+	
F	D	C	B	A	GRADE

PowerPoint Travel Commercial Rubric

Name: **Date:**

Standards:		Beginning	Developing	Accomplished	Exemplary Extension	
		1	2	3	4	Score
CRITERIA	**Content**	Includes a title, a mentioning of two or less areas of interest; but no mention of location or explanation of the cost of visiting	Includes a title and lists a few areas of interest with no description; but no explanation of the location or explanation of cost of visiting	Includes a title, a description of and significance of the areas of interest, a description of and explanation of the significance of the location, and an explanation of the cost of visiting	Along with all the elements of #3, includes a catchy slogan or twist that will lure customers in	
	Professionalism	Includes at least 5 slides, with at least 2 animated graphics from an outside source	Includes at least 8 slides, with at least 5 animated graphics from an outside source	Includes at least 10 slides, 1 animated graphic on each slide from an outside source, and at least 1 advanced feature such as sound or video	Along with all the elements of #3, includes an audio narration that accompanies each slide	
	Mechanics	Includes more than 5 grammatical errors, misspellings, or punctuation errors	Includes 1-4 grammatical errors, misspellings, or punctuation errors	Correct grammar, spelling, punctuation, and capitalization ; no errors in text	No errors in text; contains complex sentences with varied word choice	

Comments:

Total points

Grade

"Problem of the Week" Binder Rubric

Name:

Date:

CRITERIA	1	2	3	4	5/EXTENSION
Organization	• Binder does not exist	• Has binder • 5 or fewer problems in binder	• Has binder • 14 or more problems • Disorganized; problems out of order	• Has binder • All 18 problems • Organized by date	• All 18 problems in binder • Neatly labeled and organized • Table of contents
Method of Solution	• Does not provide methods of solution	• Most solutions show little understanding of problems • Barely communicates solutions	• Shows partial but limited solutions • Does not communicate solutions clearly or completely	• Communicates solutions to problems clearly	• Communicates solutions clearly and accurately using charts, graphs, symbols, and written explanations
Understanding of Problems	• No problems	• Shows little understanding of the problems	• Shows partial understanding of the problems	• Shows an essential grasp of the central ideas in the problem	• Show full grasp of the central ideas in all the problems
Neatness	• Problems are written on bits of paper in pen	• Problems are scribbled on notebook paper in pen • Much of work is not legible	• Problems are printed on notebook paper in pencil • Some work is not legible	• Problems are neatly written in pencil • Binder contains only legible work	• Problems are neatly written in pencil with accompanying diagrams neatly drawn • All work is legible with no stray marks
Points					
Total points				**Grade**	

PROOFREADER'S CHECKLIST

Writer's Name: ______________________________

Title of Work: ______________________________

Editor/s: ________________________________

Circle **Yes** or **No** after each area you proofread.

1.	All sentences begin with a capital letter.	Yes	No
2.	All sentences end with the proper punctuation mark.	Yes	No
3.	All proper names begin with a capital letter.	Yes	No
4.	All words are spelled correctly.	Yes	No
5.	There are no missing words.	Yes	No
6.	There are no extra words.	Yes	No
7.	Commas are used properly.	Yes	No
8.	Apostrophes are used properly.	Yes	No
9.	Quotation marks are used properly.	Yes	No
10.	All words are spaced properly.	Yes	No
11.	Paragraphs are used properly.	Yes	No
12.	The paper is neat and legible.	Yes	No

READ ALOUD RUBRIC

Name: **Date:**

Standards:

CRITERIA		1	2	3	
	Expression	read in a monotone voice; lacks expression when reading when reading	read with some expression to enhance reading for audience	read with great expression that enhanced reading for audience	PUBLIC SPEAKER
	Volume	low volume; listener struggles to hear	medium voice; listener able to hear yet still a bit difficult	strong voice, great volume; listener can hear clearly without difficulty	SPORTS ANNOUNCER
	Flow	reads with choppy flow and too fast or too slow a pace	good smooth speed but choppy; or smooth flow but too fast or slow a pace	nice steady pace and a nice smooth flow	SMOOTH
	Decoding	unable to use phonic rules to sound out unfamiliar word	able to use phonic rules but unable to pronounce unfamiliar word correctly	using phonic rules to sound out unfamiliar word and to pronounce it correctly	GREAT DETECTIVE
	Following Sentences	reader jumps sentences, adds or deletes words, and repeats words	reader adds or deletes words or repeats words	reader completes text as presented on the page	RIGHT ON TRACK
	Points				
	Total points				

Comments:

Ratings

15 = Master Reader
10 = Working On It
5 = Needs Practice

RESEARCH PAPER RUBRIC

Name:

Date:

Standards:	Absent	NSH	OK	Good	Excellent	
	0	1	2	3	4	5
CRITERIA						
INTRODUCTION • presents the problem/topic • explains why the problem/topic was chosen						
BODY • main ideas with supporting details • objective language • accurate information in your own words						
CONCLUSION • brief • summarizes major point/s • reasonable; supported by evidence						
REFERENCES • complete listing of resources • correct bibliographic format						
FORMAT • cover sheet • title page • introduction, body, conclusion • bibliography						
CONVENTIONS (MECHANICS) • correct spelling • correct grammar and punctuation • complete sentences						
APPEARANCE (NEATNESS) • legible letter forms • effective word and letter spacing • clean corrections • borrowed illustrations neatly trimmed						

Comments:

0	1	8	15	22	
	2-6	9-13	16-20	23-27	
	7	14	21	28+	
F	D	C	B	A	GRADE

RUBRIC FOR ROCKETRY UNIT

Name: **Date:**

Standards:

CRITERIA		Fair 1	Good 2	Excellent 3	Superior 4
C R I T E R I A	**Construction** • parts • labels • key	Most of the parts are on the model rocket, but labels are missing	Each part of model rocket is present, but labels are missing	Each part of model rocket is present and labeled	Each part of the model rocket is present, labeled, and defined on a separate key
	Appearance • parts • colors	None of the parts that are on the model are colored	Most of the parts on the model are colored	All parts from model rocket kit are used and colored	All parts from model rocket kit are used and colored, including advanced motor parts and additional equipment
	Creativity • new colors • new symbols	Not all labels or colors are used; no additional colors or symbols are added	Colors and labels from kit used; only 1 different symbol added to rocket	Colors and labels from kit used; 2 different symbols are added to rocket	More than 3 additional different labels, symbols, or colors not defined in rocket kit are used
	Careers Paper	Finished rocket but no research paper	Builds rocket and writes partial research paper on rockets with no career focus	Builds rocket with necessary parts and researches one career in rocket industry	Builds superior rocket, researches a particular career associated with the rocket industry, and draws a future rocket
	Overall Presentation • launch • explanation	Successful launch with no explanation of launch	Successful launch with good explanation of launch	Successful launch with an excellent explanation	Successful launch with detailed, engaging discussion of that particular rocket and why its launch worked
	Points				
	Total points			**Grade**	

Comments:

20	A+
15 - 19	A
10 - 14	B
5 - 9	C

Science Report Rubric

Name: Date:

Standards:

C R I T E R I A		Absent 0	NSH 1	OK 2	Good 3	Excellent 4	5
	ORGANIZATION • follows proper narrative composition format						
	CONTENT • reflects accurate knowledge of topic						
	• explores 3 different aspects of the topic						
	WRITTEN TEXT • must be in your own words • follows conventions						
	BIBLIOGRAPHY • at least 2 different types of sources used						
	• correctly written in APA format						
	CONVENTIONS (MECHANICS) • correct spelling • correct grammar and punctuation • correct paragraph structures						
	APPEARANCE (NEATNESS) • legible letter forms • effective word and letter spacing • clean corrections						

Comments:

0	1 2-7 8	9 10-15 16	17 18-23 24	25 26-31 32+	
F	D	C	B	A	GRADE

SHORT STORY RUBRIC

Name:

Date:

Standards:

CRITERIA	Absent 0	NSH 1	OK 2	Good 3	Excellent 4	Excellent 5
INTRODUCTION • good beginning • arouses interest						
BODY • develops plot with complications, consequences, and climax						
ENDING • satisfactory; no "loose ends" • problem is open-ended and interpretive						
SETTING • specific • creates visual and auditory images						
MOOD • creates an overall feeling						
CHARACTERS • appropriate • developed both physically and emotionally						
CONVENTIONS (MECHANICS) • correct spelling • correct grammar & punctuation • complete sentences						
APPEARANCE (NEATNESS) • legible letter forms • effective word & letter spacing • clean corrections						

Comments:

0	1 2-7 8	9 10-15 16	17 18-23 24	25 26-31 32+	
F	D	C	B	A	GRADE

SOFTWARE GAME RUBRIC

Standards:

Name: Date:

CRITERIA	1	2	3	4	5/EXTENSION
Software Development • Ease of use • Page linkage	• Game does not load an/or run • None of the pages link	• Game "freezes up" frequently • Some pages do not link	• Games "freezes up" on occasion • Most pages link, but sometimes incorrectly	• Game does not "freeze up" • All pages link appropriately	• Game runs quickly and flawlessly • Pages link quickly and appropriately
Game Design • Clarity of instructions • Logical steps in game • Creativity	• No instructions • No apparent steps • No evident creativity	• Instructions available but not clearly presented • Steps with little logic • Creative use of some design elements • Game plan similar to others	• Instructions available in a handout • Game is logically understandable • Creative use of design elements • Game plan has a slightly different approach than others	• Instructions available in handout and in software • Game is easy to understand • Clever game plan uses design elements creatively	• Instructions are concisely and clearly presented via software and handout • Superbly written steps • Original, elaborate game plan • Dramatic, creative use of design elements
Content • Reflects topic • Age appropriate • Accuracy • Interest level	• Does not reflect topic • Does not hold interest	• Content is too elementary but on assigned topic • Much information is inaccurate • Confusing for user	• Age appropriate material on topic • Most information is accurate • Keeps the user's interest	• Information is age appropriate, accurate, and interesting • User enjoys playing the game	• Game is engaging, challenging, and informative • User is motivated to play game repeatedly
Verbal Explanation of Game • Verbal presentation • Eye contact • Presence	• No eye contact • Does not verbal presentation	• Limited eye contact • Verbal presentation cannot be heard by audience	• Eye contact is made • Verbal presentation is clear	• Good eye contact • Speaks clearly and projects • Acknowledges audience	• Outstanding body language and eye contact • Moves confidently through audience • Engaging presentation
Points					
	Total points			**Grade**	

SOUND IDENTIFICATION AND RECOGNITION RUBRIC

Name: Date:

Standards:		1 Point	2 Points	3 Points
CRITERIA	**Beginning Sounds**	Unable to identify and recognize beginning letter sounds accurately	Identifies and recognizes beginning single consonant and vowel sounds	Identifies and recognizes beginning single, double, and triple consonant sounds
	Middle Sounds	Unable to identify and recognize middle letter sounds accurately	Identifies and recognizes single middle vowel and consonant sounds	Identifies and recognizes single, double, and triple middle vowel and consonant sounds
	Ending Sounds	Unable to identify and recognize ending letter sounds accurately	Identifies and recognizes ending single vowel and consonant sounds	Identifies and recognizes single, double, and triple ending vowel and consonant sounds

Comments:

SCORING

Points	Description
9	Exceeds Expectation
7 – 8	Excellent
5 – 6	Satisfactory
3 – 4	Needs Improvement

CREATE A SPIDER RUBRIC

Name: **Date:**

Standards:		1	2	3	4	5 Extension
CRITERIA	**Spider has correct number of body parts**	Spider is not completed	Spider has only one body part	Spider has two body parts, but no fangs or face	Spider has all body parts including fangs and face	Spider has all body parts and resembles real spider
	Spider has correct number of legs	Spider has no legs	Spider has four legs	Spider has six legs	Spider has eight legs	Spider has eight segmented legs
	Student made a drawing of the spider	No drawing is done	Drawing does not resemble spider	Drawing is done but not colored	Drawing is done with color	Drawing uses bright colors and mirrors spider
	Student used creative materials to make spider	Spider is not completed	All the same materials are used; no diversity	A variety of materials are used	A variety of materials are used creatively	Unusual materials are used creatively
	Points					
	Total points				**Grade**	

Comments:

STOCK MARKET UNIT RUBRIC

Standards:

Name:

Date:

CRITERIA	1	2	3	4	5/EXTENSION
Organization • Notebook • Transaction Records • Notes • Legible	• 3 or less records of transactions • No order • Sloppy • Notes missing • No additional material	• 4 transactions • Most notes kept in sequential order • Not all notes are legible	• 5 transactions • All notes kept and in order • Legible • No additional material •	• All transactions included • All notes in order • Neat • Some additional material included	• All of 4 • Charts and graphs with interpretations of stocks • Stock articles
Computation Skills • Calculations using percentages • Keeping balances	• Computations that are shown are not legible or are incorrect	• Most computations are correct • Not all are shown • Sloppy	• All required computations are included • 90% are correct • Legible	• All computations are included • All are correct • Neat • In order	• All of 4 • Comparison of 5% savings account vs. stock increase or decrease
Navigating the Internet • Market research • Market transactions	• Can access stock program site • Cannot make transactions	• Can make transactions • Can access most stock program tools	• Makes transactions • Uses all tools within stock program site	• Same as 3 • Has found additional sites for research	• Same as 4 • Has discovered Web sites that were used for stock selection • Noted how and why
Paper • Understanding of capitalism • Pros and cons of investing	• Gave definition of capitalism • Did not offer any type of evaluation	• Defined capitalism • Gave one pro and one con	• Capitalism explained • Several examples given for and against	• Same as 3 • Examples of different types of investment given	• Same as 4 • Examination of a Communist economy • Comparison of Communist and capitalist economies
Points					
	Total points			**Grade**	

Story Rubric

Standards:

Name: Date:

CRITERIA	1	2	3	4	5
Structure/ Organization	Unorganized main idea and details.	Attempted main idea with supporting details.	Clear main idea but details are unclear. Obvious attempt.	Organization is strong. Good main idea and supporting details. Has a beginning, middle, and end.	Well organized with main idea, details, and concluding sentence. Clear beginning, middle, and end.
Spelling/ Grammar	Very difficult to read because of spelling and grammar mistakes.	Many errors. Reader has a difficult time understanding the meaning.	Five or less grammar and spelling errors. Obvious awareness.	Minimal errors that do not disrupt fluency.	Errors that do not disrupt fluency.
Fluency	Lack of order and unable to follow idea.	Attempted order but transitions are unclear.	Transitions are not fluent, but do not hinder the reader.	Created a clear picture that flows well.	Well developed. Created excellent transitions and cohesiveness.
Descriptive Language	Descriptive language is very vague or completely absent.	Very few adjectives and not well developed.	Provided adjectives that included colorful and descriptive words.	Included a variety of descriptive language which created enjoyment for the reader.	Rich with vivid and imaginative words and language. The reader could easily envision the details.
Points					
Total points				Grade	

Comments:

Time Capsule Rubric

Standards:

Name: Date:

CRITERIA	1	2	3	4	5/EXTENSION
Time Capsule • Colorful • Creatively designed • Two-shoebox size	• Capsule is not colorful or creative • Does not follow size guidelines	• Capsule is colorful and/or creatively designed • Does not follow size guidelines	• Capsule is colorful and/or creatively designed • Follows size guidelines	• Capsule is colorful and detailed with creative designs • Follows size guidelines	• Capsule is creatively colored and detailed with elaborate designs • Follows size guidelines
Verbal Presentation • Speaks clearly • Projects voice well • Addresses audience	• Does not speak clearly, project voice, or address the audience	• Does not speak clearly or project voice • Addresses the audience	• Speaks clearly • Projects voice • Addresses the audience	• Speaks clearly with good voice projection • Focus on audience • Maintains audience attention	• Addresses audience clearly; excellent voice projection • Demonstrates confidence • Maintains audience attention
Letter • Purpose of capsule • Introduction and conclusion • Explanations of capsule items	• Purpose of time capsule is not clear • No introduction, conclusion, or explanations	• Purpose of time capsule is clear • Explanations are not consistent • Introduction and conclusion unclear	• Purpose is clearly stated • Explanations are consistent • Clear introduction and conclusion	• Purpose is clearly stated • Explanations are detailed • Clear introduction and conclusion	• Purpose is stated elaborately • Introduction and conclusion are clear and flow smoothly • Detailed explanations
Capsule Items • Reflect community • Demonstrate 100 years of passing time	• Do not reflect community • Do not show 100 years of passing time	• Reflect community • Do not show 100 years of passing time	• Reflect community • Demonstrate 100 years of passing time	• Variety of items • Reflect community • Show progression of time	• Extensive number of items • Reflect community • Show progression of time over consecutive years
Points					
	Total points			Grade	

TOOTHPICK BRIDGE RUBRIC

Name: **Date:**

Standards:

CRITERIA		Absent 0	NSH 2	OK 4	Good 6	Excellent 8	Excellent 10
C	**APPEARANCE** • attractive design • neatly constructed						
R I	**BRIDGE PLANS** • finished bridge matches design plans						
T	**CODE** • meets specifications of size and dimensions						
E	**RECORD KEEPING** • accuracy • completeness						
R	**FUNDS** • money used to purchase materials: $________________						
I A	**OVERALL STRENGTH** • holds: ______________ grams						

Comments:

0	1-3 4-9 10-12	13-15 16-21 21-24	25-27 28-33 34-36	37-39 40-46 47+	
F	D	C	B	A	GRADE

Travel Brochure Rubric 1

Standards:

Name: Date:

Criteria	1	2	3	4	5/Extension
Contents • Residential areas • Commercial areas • Recreational areas • Historical areas • Pictures/photos	• Different areas not indicated • No pictures or photos	• Does not have information on each area • A few photos or pictures are included	• Has information about each area • Does not have pictures or photos for each area	• Has a lot of information about each area • Has pictures and/or photos for each area	• Contains in-depth information about each area • Expressive photos and/or pictures
Format • Separate sections • Title • Headings	• Sections not clearly marked or titled	• Sections not clearly marked • Main title only	• Sections clearly marked with headings • Main title evident	• Sections distinctly marked • Title and headings evident	• Sections are distinguished in a creative manner • Creative title and headings
Map • Locations of different areas • Map scale • Compass rose	• Locations of areas not shown • No scale or rose	• Locations shown • No scale or rose	• Locations shown • Map scale defined • Has a compass rose	• Area locations are detailed • Map scale defined • Has a compass rose	• Provides true reflection of areas • Creative compass rose • Map scale is defined
Appearance • Folded 8.5x11 paper • Design elements • Colorful • Neat • Legible	• Not proper size • No design elements • Not colorful • Not neat • Not legible	• Proper size • Colorful • Neat • Not legible • No consistent design plan	• Not proper size • Design plan evident • Colorful • Neat • Legible	• Proper size • Consistent use of design elements throughout • Colorful • Neat • Legible	• Proper size • Colorful throughout • Creatively designed • Neat • Legible • Unique elements • Ready for travel agency
Points					
Total points				**Grade**	

Travel Brochure Rubric 2

Standards:

Name: Date:

CRITERIA		1	2	3	4	5/Extension	Points	
C R	**Contents** • Residential areas • Commercial areas • Recreational areas • Historical areas • Pictures/photos	• Different areas not indicated • No pictures or photos	• Does not have information on each area • A few photos or pictures are included	• Has information about each area • Does not have pictures/photos for each area	• Has a lot of information about each area • Has pictures for each area	• Contains in-depth information about each area • Expressive photos/pictures	x10	
I T	**Format** • Separate sections • Title • Headings	• Sections not clearly marked or titled	• Sections not clearly marked • Main title only	• Sections clearly marked with headings • Main title evident	• Sections distinctly marked • Title and headings evident	• Sections are distinguished in a creative manner • Creative title and headings	x4	
E R	**Map** • Locations of different areas • Map scale • Compass rose	• Locations of areas not shown • No scale or rose	• Locations shown • No scale or rose	• Locations shown • Map scale defined • Has a compass rose	• Area locations are detailed • Map scale defined • Has a compass rose	• Provides true reflection of areas • Creative compass rose • Map scale is defined	x5	
I A	**Appearance** • Folded 8.5x11 paper • Design elements • Colorful • Neat • Legible	• Not proper size • No design elements • Not colorful • Not neat • Not legible	• Proper size • Colorful • Neat • Not legible • No consistent design plan	• Not proper size • Design plan evident • Colorful • Neat • Legible	• Proper size • Consistent use of design elements throughout • Colorful • Neat • Legible	• Proper size • Colorful throughout • Creatively designed • Neat • Legible • Unique elements • Ready for travel agency	x6	

Grade: ______ Total points: ______

RUBRIC FOR TRIGONOMETRIC GRAPHS

Name: **Date:**

Standards:

		Fair 1	Good 2	Excellent 3	Score
CRITERIA	**Amplitude, Period, and Phase Shift** Correctly identified	One component identified correctly	2 of 3 components identified correctly	All 3 components identified correctly	
	Horizontal Axis Labeled	Scale present but incorrect	Scale present with only endpoints identified	Scale clear, precise with 4 or 5 points correctly identified	
	Cycle One shown correctly	Cycle present but inaccurate	Cycle present with only one characteristic incorrect or the graph follows from student's attributes	Cycle present and accurate in all attributes	
	Description Of procedures taken	Phrases or facts stated	Sentences used to describe steps (which are accurate)	Complete explanation describing the use of characteristics to determine the graph	
	Original Problem Original problem that can be solved using the equation and graph	Indicates an area which is harmonic and uses trig functions	Characteristics of problem reflect amplitude, period, and/or phase shift	Problem is consistent with attributes and demonstrates understanding and creativity	

Comments:

Total points

Grade

TV News Show Rubric

Team Names: Date:

Standards:

CRITERIA	Absent	NSH	OK	Good	Excellent	
	0	1	2	3	4	5
INTERNATIONAL NEWS Visual Aid:						
STATE NEWS Visual Aid:						
LOCAL NEWS Visual Aid:						
SPORTS Visual Aid:						
SPECIAL NEWS ITEM Visual Aid:						
WEATHER Visual Aid:						
COMMERCIAL 1 Visual Aid:						
COMMERCIAL 2 Visual Aid:						
TOTAL PRESENTATION LENGTH:						

Comments:

0	1-4	18-21	35-38	52-55	
	5-13	22-30	39-47	56-64	
	14-17	31-34	48-51	65+	
F	D	C	B	A	GRADE

VETERAN'S DAY DOLL RUBRIC

Standards:

Name: Date:

CRITERIA	1	2	3	4	5/EXTENSION
Doll Dimensions • Made of paper • 1 foot x 1 foot • Proportional body parts	• Not made of paper • Not correct size • Body parts are not proportional	• Made of paper • Not correct size • Body parts are not proportional	• Made of paper • Correct size but body parts are not proportional; OR • Parts proportional but wrong size	• All criteria met • Followed all instructions	
Information Card • Provides details • Explanation about branch of service	• Details not given • No explanation	• Details not given • Poorly written explanation	• Few details given • Nicely written explanation	• Many details given • Well written explanation	• Details are extensive • Explanation provides in-depth understanding
Doll Representation • U.S. military service • Reflects rank in military • Proper costume • Badges • Rank insignia • Nametag	• Does not reflect a military service person • Does not show rank in service; no badge, rank insignia, nametag	• Represents a service person • Costume has some but not all of these: badge, rank insignia, nametag • May not reflect rank in service	• Represents a service person • Represents rank in the service • Costume has badge, rank insignia, and nametag	• Represents a service person • Costume has necessary badges to reflect rank • Costume has additional details that reflect a soldier	• Doll reflects a specific area of military service • Costume has all symbols to reflect rank and other possible details • Costume reflects a variety of military levels
Points					

Total points: ______ **Grade**: ______

WEB SITE DESIGN RUBRIC

Standards:

Name: Date:

CRITERIA	Level 1	Level 2	Level 3	Level 4	Level 5 EXTENSION
Layout	Layout has no structure or organization	Text broken into paragraphs and/or sections	Headings and sections are labeled and create hierarchy; some consistency	Hierarchy closely follows meaning; heading and styles are consistent within pages	Consistent format extends page-to-page; text, images, and links flow together
Writing Mechanics	Difficult to understand; some spelling and other errors	Many errors but consistent line of thought	Easy to understand; some spelling and grammar errors	Easy to understand; few spelling and grammar errors	Clear, concise, and well written with no spelling and grammar errors
Images	Images are unrelated to page	One image with some relation to page and text	Three images with some relation to page and text	Four images with strong relation to text and page; images are from 2 or more sources	Five or more images with strong relation to text and pages; images have proper size, colors, and cropping; images are from 3 or more sources (Scan, PhotoShop, Video, Photo Deluxe, etc.)
Network	Student has problems bringing up his or her Web page within a Web browser	Text is in a program other than the word processor; one or more files in wrong location	Some files in simple word processor of HTML	Most files in simple word processor of HTML	All files in simple word processor of HTML; efficient use of Internet access programs

Comments:

WORKING TOGETHER
IN A COOPERATIVE GROUP

Project or Unit: ______________________________

Rate your group according to the following scale:

1 = We didn't do this at all
2 = We need a lot of help in this
3 = We did well with this
4 = We were outstanding in this ____________

Commitment to Purpose .... Group Rating _____

Interest in task
Motivation to complete assignment
Followed directions

Work Process Group Rating .... Group Rating _____

Everyone participated
We didn't waste time
Ideas built on one another

Decision Making .... Group Rating _____

Looked for solutions all could accept
Followed orderly process in making decisions
Decisions were not forced on some people

Communication .... Group Rating _____

Listened to all suggestions
We stayed on task in discussions
Our talking did not disturb the class

Creativity .... Group Rating _____

Considered new ways of doing things
Brainstormed ideas
No put-downs for different thinking

Conflict .... Group Rating _____

Established rules for dealing with conflict
Avoided personal attacks
Examined different points of view

Leadership .... Group Rating _____

Group decided on leadership tasks and roles
Everyone took some responsibility
Group leader was fair to all

Group Members: ______________________________

Writers' Workshop Rubric

Name: Date:

Standards:

CRITERIA	Absent	NSH	Good	Excellent	
	0	1	2	3	4
Used writing log	not at all	some of the time	much of the time	nearly all of the time	always writing in log
Drafts kept in folder	no drafts in folder	some drafts in folder	most drafts in folder	all drafts in folder	
Finished three final drafts 3 different types of writing	no final drafts	one final draft	two final drafts; 2 different kinds of writing	three final drafts; 3 different kinds of writing	more than 3 final drafts reflecting at least 3 kinds of writing
Daily attitude	negative and distracting	OK, but sometimes distracting	good, and not distracting	positive and focused	positive and supportive of others
Daily effort	wrote nothing	wrote very little	wrote much of the time	wrote most of the time	spent every available moment writing
Points					
Total points			Grade		

Comments:

13 - 15		A
10 - 12		B
7 - 9		C
4 - 6		D
0 - 3		F

WRITING ASSESSMENT RUBRIC

Name:

Standards:

Date:

CRITERIA		1	2	3	4
C	CONTENT	• lack of focus • little, if any, organization • limited or unclear supporting ideas • development limited to repetition of key words	• controlling idea unclear or minimal develop. • multiple controlling ideas. None developed • ideas are few, general, or irrelevant • organization overwhelms development • sense of completeness lacking	• clear controlling idea • uneven develop. of beginning, middle, & end • generally relevant supporting ideas • ideas presented with logical connections • appropriate organization • sense of completeness	• strong, clear controlling idea • even development of beginning, middle, & end • even development of main & supporting ideas • ideas supported with examples & details • appropriate, logical organization • sense of completeness/fullness
R I	STYLE	• lack of engaging, precise, or varied language • flat or inappropriate tone • lack of transitions • no awareness of audience • lack of individuality/voice • lack of original student writing	• little engaging, precise, or varied language • impersonal, inconsistent, or uneven tone • approach inconsistent with purpose • transitions inappropriate or overused • little awareness of audience • little individuality/voice • limited original student writing	• generally precise or engaging language • appropriate tone for audience & purpose • approach suited to topic & purpose • consistent awareness of audience • transitions linking ideas & parts of paper • some sense of writer's individuality/voice • sufficient original student writing	• precise or engaging language • varied word choice • appropriate tone that is strong • interesting presentation & complete info • transitions lead the reader • clear sense of voice or individuality • extensive original student writing
T E	SENTENCES	• sentence-level meaning confused • frequent use of fragments & run-ons • too few sentences • end punctuation missing or incorrect	• mixture of effective/ineffective, clear/confused sentences • competence in complete simple sentences • end punctuation correct & incorrect	• clear, effective sentences • elements within sentences joined correctly • variety in length & type of sentences • generally correct end punctuation • competence in either coordination or subordination	• consistent clarity of meaning • correct end punctuation • extensive variety of sentences • variety of subordination & coordination • repetition for effect
R I	USAGE	• severe & repeated errors in subject-verb agreement, word forms, pronoun reference • usage errors that create a barrier to understanding	• a mixture of correct & incorrect instances of usage • competence in one or two components	• subject-verb agreement • correct noun & verb formation • clear pronoun reference • correct word forms • some variety in all components	• singular and plural subject-verb agreement • correct use of varied pronouns • correct & complete word forms • ability to manipulate the conventions of usage for effect • variety of contexts & instances in all components
A	MECHANICS	• meaning obscured by severity & frequency of errors	• mechanics used correctly in some contexts • competence in one or two components	• limited # of errors in one or more components • correct instances in each component present • components not demonstrated in a wide variety of contexts	• components demonstrated in a wide variety of instances & contexts • occasional proofreading errors • manipulation of mechanics for effect

CONTENT SCORE: ____ X 3 = ____ SENTENCE SCORE: ____ USAGE SCORE: ____

STYLE SCORE: ____ X 2 = ____ MECHANICS SCORE: ____ **TOTAL SCORE: ____**

Writing Rubric

Name: ______________________ Date: ______________

Title: ______________________ Editing Partner/s: ______________

----- FOCUS -----

1	2	3	4	5	6
Absent	Confused	Vague	Adequate	Clear	Sharp, distinct

----- CONTENT -----

1	2	3	4	5	6
Absence of relevant content	Superficial	Limited to a listing, repetition, or mere sequence of ideas	Sufficient	Specific and illustrative	Substantial, specific &/or illustrative content with well-developed, sophisticated ideas

----- ORGANIZATION -----

1	2	3	4	5	6
Absent	Confused	Inconsistent	Appropriate	Logical and appropriate	Obviously controlled

----- STYLE -----

1	2	3	4	5	6
No control of word choice or sentence structure	Lack of sentence and word choice	Limited sentence variety and word choice	Some precision & variety in word choice and sentence structure	Precision and variety in sentence structure and word choice	Tone apparent in sentence structure & word choice

----- CONVENTIONS -----

1	2	3	4	5	6
Errors so severe that ideas are too hard to understand	Errors seriously interfere with purpose	Repeated weaknesses	Errors do not interfere significantly with purpose	Some mechanical and usage errors	Few mechanical and usage errors

Teacher's Comments:

25 - 30	=	A
20 - 24	=	B
10 - 19	=	C
5 - 9	=	D
0 - 4	=	E

Total Points: ______________

Grade: ______________